on track ...
Warren Zevon

every album, every song

Peter Gallagher

sonicbondpublishing.com

Sonicbond Publishing Limited
www.sonicbondpublishing.co.uk
Email: info@sonicbondpublishing.co.uk

First Published in the United Kingdom 2022
First Published in the United States 2022

British Library Cataloguing in Publication Data:
A Catalogue record for this book is available from the British Library

ISBN 978-1-78952-170-2

Typeset in ITC Garamond & ITC Avant Garde
Printed and bound in England

Graphic design and typesetting: Full Moon Media

on track ...
Warren Zevon

every album, every song

Peter Gallagher

sonicbondpublishing.com

Thanks always to Annie. You are El Amor de Mi Vida.

I became a lifelong Zevonista in 1978. It was my brother Paul's fault.

This book's for him.

on track ...

Warren Zevon

Contents

Introduction

Renfrew, Scotland. A Friday evening, one of the five in October 1978. I can narrow it down to a Friday, because my brother Paul always visited friends in Clydebank, the town in which my family had previously lived, on a Thursday night, and he regularly returned from this jaunt with a selection of borrowed albums, a simple, communal and once-common pleasure rendered obsolete in the Spotify age. So here I am the following day, school long over, dinner done and dusted, flipping through the trio of long players recommended by one or other of Paul's mates.

It may be a cliché, but those pesky mists of time long ago made off with the identity of the first album. Try as I might, I can't remember, and as someone that alphabetises their record collection, you can rest assured I have tried. Many times. My mind's eye has proven to be pretty rubbish at conjuring forth that elusive cover art. I can only assume I was unfamiliar with the act or artist, and that nothing about the cover art or song titles elicited curiosity.

The second record was entitled *Excitable Boy* by someone called Warren Zevon, a name that meant nothing to me, so it too was quickly cast aside in favour of the third album, Jackson Browne's *Running on Empty*. I had really enjoyed Browne's previous record *The Pretender,* and had been particularly dazzled by its title track, which remains my favourite Browne song (Decades later, I read that the songwriter had been trying to ape this Zevon guy's style when he wrote it). I also appreciated Browne's take on the old Zodiacs hit 'Stay', the singer's only British hit single, which reached number 12 in the UK in the summer of '78. It was a no-brainer that *Running on Empty* was getting first spin.

Running on Empty was subsequently to become one of my favourite Browne recordings. It's a clever piece of work, a concept album about 'the road' and touring, recorded live in hotel rooms, on the tour bus, backstage and onstage. This approach surely makes it unique amongst live rock albums, as does the decision to include only new material, some of which – the title track, 'Rosie', and 'The Load-Out' with that seamless transition into 'Stay' – easily holds its own against the best of Browne's studio work.

However, I never got to hear *Running on Empty* in its entirety that October night, for I was unsettled by a presence in the room. Directly opposite, sitting on the floor by the stereo, staring out from a 12" by 12" crimson-coloured card, was that Zevon fella. And frankly, he was creeping me out. Is that boy smiling or snarling? Are the teeth peeking through those slightly parted lips razor-sharp and fanged? Is that dude wearing lipstick? And worst of all, why did he have to have those psycho eyes that follow you around the room? This guy had gone from looking like a choirboy to a serial killer in the space of three Jackson Browne songs, and I was intrigued. I flipped the sleeve over to look at the song titles and was hooked further. I had no idea what 'Johnny Strikes Up The Band' sounded like, but what a brilliant title for an opening track. As an old Universal horror film buff, it went without saying that a song called 'Werewolves Of

London' warranted further investigation. And what did that brilliant phrase 'Accidentally Like A Martyr' even *mean*? But the title that most screamed for my attention was the second track, 'Roland The Headless Thompson Gunner'. I couldn't even imagine what genre of music such an oddly titled song belonged to, but it convinced me I *had* to be playing this album, not next, but right now. *Running on Empty* would need to wait another day, although, as I was about to learn, Browne was a major presence on *Excitable Boy*, co-producing, co-authoring one song, and singing harmonies on several others.

'Johnny Strikes Up The Band' indeed proved to be an effective album opener, but, much as he was to do with his nemesis Van Owen, it was 'Roland the Headless Thompson Gunner' that blew me away. I had never encountered a song like it, a macabre tale of grisly revenge from beyond the grave, encompassing history, geography, current affairs and politics. When the song ended, I sat in shell-shocked silence before lifting the arm of the record player and putting the needle back at the beginning, doing this several times over until I had learned the lyrics by heart. I was so struck by this modern horror story that I wasn't yet ready to listen to the rest of the album. So I took my dog out for a walk in the dark and the drizzle and let 'Roland' replay in my head.

On my return, I played *Excitable Boy* in its entirety and loved it enough to quickly invest in my own copy. A quick check of the shelves of the Listen record shop in nearby Paisley informed me that Zevon had released a self-titled album two years earlier, so now it was a matter of saving my pennies. Thereafter, I bought every Warren Zevon album on its day of release, right up until his final effort *The Wind*.

So, I am a fan, guilty as charged, but hopefully, one free of unfettered fawning and sycophancy. As you will see, there are several Zevon albums that I think are classics, but I don't think he has a single one where *every* track is a winner. He was a master of inconsistency, and for every masterpiece like 'Roland', there were lesser songs, some maudlin, some twee, some just downright bland. Which is which in the pages that follow is a matter of opinion, specifically mine, and you are welcome to disagree with some or all of them, but hopefully, you will at least agree they have been objectively formed.

What Is Included In This Book?

The primary focus is on the twelve studio albums and the two official live documents, *Stand in the Fire* and *Learning to Flinch*. The studio material is in the order of recording, not order of release. Thus, *The First Sessions* – which was not released until 2003 – comes first, as it presents Zevon's earliest recorded work. Several compilations are included, such as *I'll Sleep When I'm Dead*, which includes some noteworthy previously unreleased tracks from Zevon's television soundtrack work, *The First Sessions*, which collects his early work with lyme and cybelle, and *Preludes: Rare and Unreleased Recordings*, which contains archival material, including alternative versions of later songs and some unheard songs seeing their first light of day.

The First Sessions (2003)

Personnel:
Warren Zevon: vocals; guitar and bass on '(You Used to) Ride So High'
Violet Santangelo: vocals
Tommy Tedesco, Dennis Budimir: guitars
Lyle Ritz: bass
Larry Knetchel: piano, organ
Hal Blaine: drums
Bones Howe: percussion; drums and percussion on '(You Used to) Ride So High'
Lenny Malarsky, Joe DiFiore, Joe Saxon, Jessie Erlich: string quartet on 'Like The Seasons'
Joe Osborn: bass on 'If You Gotta Go, Go Now'
Ollie Mitchell, Jules Chaiken, Dick Leith, Lou Blackburn: brass on 'If You Gotta Go, Go Now'
Producer: Bones Howe for White Whale Records, 1965-1966
Release date: March 2003
Label: Varese Sarabande
Chart placing: Did not chart
Running time: 33.34

'Stumpy' Zevon: gangster. Born William Zivotofsky, 1903, in Kyiv, Ukraine. He came to America when he was two, his family settling in Brooklyn. But Stumpy was not for settling, and when he hit his mid-teens, he was out of there. First stop, the Windy City, still in the malevolent, pudgy grip of Al Capone. Stumpy made pals in a couple of up-and-comers, Sam Giancana and Mickey Cohen, serving as the latter's best man in 1940. A decade passes, more, the itchy feet kick in. Stumpy moves west and opens a chain of carpet stores. Real business? Front? A bit of both? Doesn't really matter, for it was in 1946 in his Fresno store, amidst the wool blends, the nylon, the polyester and the polypropylene, the underlay and the tacking, that he met a girl half his 42 years.

Beverley Simmons was brought up in a devout Mormon home. Her parents watch aghast as this silver-tongued Jewish gangster woos their willing accomplice of a daughter, marries her, and hightails it back to Chicago. It's almost too perfect. Broken down into three verses and a chorus, it's ideal material for the song noir their son, born Warren William Zevon on 24 January 1947, would become known for.

It was also far from perfect. Stumpy, now in his mid-40s, had grown accustomed to a life of itinerant bachelorhood, and when the mood took him, still engaged in it. All-night gambling sessions could sometimes last longer than one night. Meanwhile, the family relocated often, and Stumpy and Beverley's relationship was no more settled. By all accounts, they were trapped in a tempestuous cycle: fight, separate, makeup, move home, fight.

Their turbulent relationship is possibly best exemplified by a chilling incident that occurred on Christmas Day 1956, when the family were back in Fresno.

Stumpy had given a delighted nine-year-old Warren an upright Chickering piano, won in an all-night Christmas Eve card game. Beverly was less delighted, and let it be known in no uncertain terms that she didn't want this 'headache machine' in her house. Stumpy's silent response was to pick up the carving knife that awaited the turkey, and hurl it at his wife. Thankfully, the blade missed its target, though reportedly not by much. Peace on Earth. Warren witnessed the entire incident. Beverly bolted to her parents' house, but it was Stumpy who left in the long term. Meanwhile, the piano stayed, and Warren set about mastering it.

Four years later, after one of their many reconciliations, Willie, Beverly and Warren were living in San Pedro, California, with Warren enrolled in Dana Junior High School. His musical ability so impressed his music teacher, that he introduced the thirteen-year-old Warren to one of the 20th century's most influential composers, Igor Stravinsky. Zevon met Stravinsky and celebrated American conductor Robert Craft no more than a handful of times, to, in Craft's recollection, 'analyse scores', but after Zevon's late-1970s success, some rock writers presented him as having been a prodigy under Stravinsky's tutelage. Zevon never promulgated this version of events, but he did admit to occasionally failing to disabuse the press of this notion. Stravinsky and Craft had a lasting impact on the young Zevon, reigniting his love of classical music, which had been in danger of being extinguished by rock and roll.

By 1964, Zevon was attending L.A.'s Fairfax High School, where he met Violet Santangelo, another Chicago emigree. Together they formed a duo called lyme and cybelle, which Zevon insisted was written lower case in the style of American poet e. e. cummings. Santangelo took her stage name from the 1962 Oscar-winning French film *Sundays and Cybele*, while Zevon's came from a brand of cologne. According to original Beach Boy David Marks, Zevon immersed himself in playing the role of stephen lyme, not only wearing his namesake aftershave, but dressing in green, wearing green-tinted glasses, and painting the walls of his apartment green.

Lyme and cybelle began performing privately for Santangelo's family and friends, and through a fortuitous connection, were soon signed to White Whale Records. Zevon also acquired a songwriting deal with publishing offshoot Ishmael Music. The duo was paired off with producer Dayton 'Bones' Howe, who had made his name engineering singles by The Mamas & The Papas and Elvis Presley, and was now co-producing White Whale's main cash cow, The Turtles. Howe would later work with The 5th Dimension, The Association, and Tom Waits.

Between 1965-1966, lyme and cybelle cut two singles for White Whale, the first a minor hit, the second a flop. By then, Zevon and Santangelo had drifted apart, largely due to the former's alcohol and drug intake, which also didn't enamour Zevon to White Whale. The record label drafted in guitarist Wayne Erwin, who had played on early Monkees singles, to be the new lyme. After one flop single, Erwin showed his gratitude by sacking Santangelo from her own band. She later became an actress, primarily in musical theatre, using the name Laura Kenyon. Meanwhile, Ishmael Music dropped Zevon as a songwriter. His first brief flirtation with fame was over.

The complete lyme and cybelle recordings and some early Zevon demos were released just prior to Zevon's death in 2003 by Varese Sarabande, a label that specialises in film and television soundtracks. The album included the two lyme and cybelle tracks with Wayne Erwin – 'Song 7' and 'Write If You Get Work' – which are not discussed here.

The First Sessions is precisely that – a collection of Zevon's earliest recordings and some unreleased demos, cobbled together and released in 2003 to cash in on the singer's newfound post-diagnosis fame as a walking dead man. He flirts with a dizzying array of styles. Garage, baroque, blues, psychedelia, folk, Broadway showstoppers and British moptop pop all vie for attention across the fully-produced tracks alone, resulting in a display more inconsistent than diverse.

Comparing this early material to Zevon's later work is an exercise in futility. These songs are too rooted in their time, as the influencing musical styles identified above make clear. The songs sound as if written by a teenager in the mid-to-late 1960s, influenced only by the music of that period. Listened to in that context, there are some enjoyable pop songs here, but anyone expecting the autobiographical, geopolitical, literary or humorous flourishes characterising Zevon's later work, will come away disappointed.

Ultimately, this collection will appeal to only the most ardent of fans, and – thanks to the bizarre inclusion of the two Wayne Erwin tracks – to that most fabled of creatures, the lyme and cybelle completist.

'Follow Me' (Santangelo, Zevon)

Whether brilliantly or inadvertently, 'Follow Me' manages to fit all the styles that defined American popular music in 1966 into its 2:30 running time. A descending bass line supports a jingle-jangly Byrdsian guitar, followed by insistent drums. Violet Santangelo takes the lead vocal, with Zevon's voice, considerably lower in the mix, entering after verse one in counter-harmony. The vocal blend nods to the sunshine pop of 'California Dreamin'', but the overall sound – especially the chorus – comes from the same garage as '96 Tears'. In short, 'Follow Me' could've been by The Mamas & The Mysterians, with a tape-melting psychedelic middle-eight thrown in for good measure. Producer Bones Howe called this single 'The first psychedelic rock record', but while its April 1966 release means it predates major psychedelic influencers such as *Pet Sounds*, *Revolver* and the first 13th Floor Elevators album, this claim conveniently overlooks many other contenders for that title, including the Byrds' 'Eight Miles High', 'See My Friends' by the Kinks, or even Joe Meek's 1960 EP I Hear a New World.

The single reached a respectable 65 on the *Billboard* pop chart, not bad for a duo that not so many weeks before were performing only for family and friends.

'Like The Seasons' (Santangelo, Zevon)

Perhaps it's just the mention of September in both songs, but 'Like The Seasons' conveys a similar autumnal melancholy to 'Try To Remember', the standout song from long-running 1960 off-Broadway musical comedy *The Fantasticks*. By serving as the flipside of the rockier 'Follow Me', this mellow slice of baroque shows the duo's versatility across the course of one single. 'Like The Seasons' is arguably strong enough to have served as the follow-up single, but the combination of both songs on one 45 makes this single an excellent representation of mid-Sixties pop.

Zevon provides the lead vocal here, and the song foreshadows the often-unexpected tenderness the singer would bring to future compositions. This was originally released minus Miss Santangelo's cowriting credit, which, if deliberate on Zevon's part, was a complete reversal of the way he operated in later life, when he could be exceptionally generous with co-crediting others.

'Like the Seasons' was recorded by The Turtles as the B-side of their 1966 single 'Can I Get to Know You Better?', which wasn't a hit. Determined to help Zevon establish his songwriting career, and against the protestations of their management, The Turtles slapped 'Like The Seasons' on the back of their following single too. 'Happy Together' fared better, topping the *Billboard* chart in March 1967. Zevon bought a white Jaguar with his royalty cheque.

'I've Just Seen A Face' (John Lennon, Paul McCartney)

This previously unreleased demo, the first of eight on this album, sounds impromptu, as if played by a boy and a girl who have stumbled upon an acoustic guitar at a party. It maintains the folky Beatles-play-Greenwich-Village feel of the original, if not the production values. This lyme and cybelle nonstarter was never intended for release, but is nonetheless worthy of inclusion in a theoretical anthology compiling the world's least essential Beatles covers.

'Peeping And Hiding' (Jimmy Reed)

When Zevon dropped Santangelo's credit from 'Like The Seasons', perhaps he was following in the footsteps of Jimmy Reed, whose songs, including this one, were (according to blues historian Gerard Herzhaft) credited to the bluesman but written by his wife Mama Reed. The 1959 Reed original was called 'Baby What You Want Me To Do', but this fully-produced, retitled and previously unreleased take is a faithful but spirited reading, with Zevon and Santangelo sharing lead vocals.

'If You Gotta Go, Go Now' (Bob Dylan)

The second lyme and cybelle single was this big, brash, brassy and thoroughly acceptable take on the 1964 Dylan song, with Zevon and Santangelo alternating verses, but it joined earlier efforts by The Liverpool Five and Manfred Mann in failing to crack the pop chart.

'I'll Go On' (Santangelo, Zevon)
The B-side of 'If You Gotta Go, Go Now' was this original ballad with its lovely vocal blend on the verses and counter-harmonising on the chorus. It's all folky and acoustic at the beginning, growing ever more ornate as it progresses, until, by the third and final verse, it's in the same baroque territory as 'Like The Seasons'. Like that song, 'I'll Go On' is arguably stronger than its A-side, with Zevon and Santangelo appearing more confident when arranging their own material. It also marked Zevon's last outing as stephen lyme.

'Follow Me' (Demo) (Santangelo, Zevon)
The vocals in this previously unreleased demo are not markedly different from those on the single version, but accompanied only by acoustic guitar, the voices are left sounding harsh, unrefined and overexposed.

'(You Used To) Ride So High' (Zevon)
Though the album sleeve identifies this as a demo, it sounds like a fully-realised single, with Bones Howe doubling on production and percussion. As a Beatles pastiche that wears its influences a mite too obviously, this unreleased slice of psychedelia captures the zeitgeist as successfully as 'Follow Me', and could've been a contender. Had it secured a release, Zevon wanted it issued under the fictitious band name The Motorcycle Abeline, which is how it is credited here.

'Outside Chance' (Glenn Crocker, Zevon)
Zevon's Beatles fan club membership card is on full display again here, as he successfully splices 'Day Tripper' and 'Ticket To Ride'. It's listed as a demo, but like the previous track, it's a fully-produced band version.

The Turtles once again championed Zevon, releasing 'Outside Chance' as an A-side. When it failed to chart, they put it on the B-side of their next single, 'Making My Mind Up', but that too was unsuccessful. Co-writer Glenn Crocker had been an early bandmate of Warren's, but when The Turtles' singles were released, his credit mysteriously suffered the same fate as Santangelo's had on the lyme and cybelle material.

'I See The Lights' (Zevon)
Another unreleased demo, but this time it sounds like it. Zevon is solo on vocal and acoustic guitar. It's a pleasant-enough mid-tempo tune, but it's hard to tell what direction it would've taken had it made it to the studio. There's a definite McCartney vibe, but equally, it sounds like it could've slotted into some contemporary hippy musical while waiting to be covered by The 5th Dimension.

'And If I Had You' (Zevon)
This paean to lost love and loneliness is like the previous lyric, but with the dreariness quota ramped up. It comes with a false ending that instils false hope, which is swiftly and brutally crushed when the song meanders on anew.

'A Bullet For Ramona' (Zevon)

This is an undated demo of the song that appeared on Zevon's 1969 debut
album *Wanted Dead or Alive*. Accompanied only by piano and handclapping,
the demo retains the country feel of the finished version.

Wanted Dead Or Alive (1970)

Personnel:
Warren Zevon: vocals, piano, guitar, bass, harmonica, marxophone, miramba, percussion
Skip Battin: bass
Drachen Theaker: drums
Jon Corneal: drums on 'Tule's Blues'; percussion on 'Fiery Emblems'
Brent Seawell: bass on 'A Bullet For Ramona'
Toxey French: drums on 'A Bullet For Ramona'
Sweet Trifles: backing vocals on 'Iko-Iko'
Recorded at Wally Heider's Studio III, San Francisco
Producer: Warren Zevon
Release Date: April 1970
Label: Liberty/Imperial
Chart placing: Did not chart
Running time: 30:58

'Are you prepared to wear black leather and chains, fuck a lot of teenage girls, and get rich?'. The clock had ticked two years past the Summer of Love, but the Age of Aquarius was still a-dawning, and the joss sticks were scented with the indelicate fragrance of macho-bullshit hedonism. And so, to the surprise of precisely no one, the respondent – one Warren Zevon – answered, 'Yes'.

The query had come from producer Kim Fowley, who in the 1970s would co-write a song called 'King Of The Night Time World', which was precisely what Fowley imagined himself to be. For now, though, he was best known as the writer and producer of a string of 1960s novelty hits, such as 'Alley-Oop' by The Hollywood Argyles, 'Papa Oom Mow Mow' by The Rivingtons and 'Nut Rocker' by B. Bumble and the Stingers.

Meanwhile, Zevon had continued writing songs, and reputedly played acoustic guitar on the title track of Phil Ochs' 1967 album *Pleasures of the Harbor*, but it was Zevon's new career as a writer of advertising jingles that was paying the bills. But hearing this work on the radio brought no satisfaction; Zevon wanted to be writing the songs his jingles were sandwiched between.

Following his ignominious departure from lyme and cybelle, Zevon decided green was unlucky, and repainted his walls and jettisoned his emerald wardrobe. Blue was the new hue of choice, and he briefly dallied with the *nom de plume* Sandy Zevon, which he thought was a cool surfer name. But this pseudonym was soon discarded, presumably when someone reminded Warren that he had a cousin called Sandy Zevon. By the time he hooked up with Fowley, he'd decided to capitalise on his striking surname, and be henceforth known mononymously as 'Zevon'.

He and Fowley were brought together through Bones Howe, who still had faith in Zevon's talent. What Howe was less certain about was himself. Perhaps he was too mainstream for the young maverick, he thought, so he hit upon the idea of pairing the songwriter with someone equally as unorthodox. Enter the first self-proclaimed Mayor of Sunset Strip.

They got on like a house that wasn't on fire. Fowley liked to call the shots and, in the 1970s, relished his role as svengali to the Hollywood Stars and The Runaways. Zevon, meanwhile, had 'Least likely to be svengalied' written under his high-school yearbook photo. The inevitable personality clash led to Fowley leaving halfway through the recording of Zevon's debut album *Wanted Dead or Alive*, and denouncing the singer as 'unproduceable'. Fowley later claimed credit for making Warren 'who he was'. In Crystal Zevon's biography of her former husband, she states Fowley as saying he 'allowed him to adopt my swagger', and told him to 'Be a prick but be a literate one'. For his part, Zevon witheringly put Fowley's departure down to the singer having 'a sudden attack of taste'.

Wanted Dead or Alive was released in 1970, features a cover shot of Zevon *sans* trademark spectacles, and, bizarrely, is dedicated to Fowley.

Calling *Wanted Dead Or Alive* a mixed bag is an understatement. At one end of the spectrum is 'Tule's Blues', a song ranking amongst his absolute best. A rung or two below, we find 'A Bullet For Ramona' and the title track, two worthwhile songs hinting at future greatness. Offset against these is an opposite end of the spectrum cluttered with 'Iko Iko', 'Gorilla' and 'Fiery Emblems', which make the album impossible to recommend, despite the luminosity of 'Tule's Blues'.

This album was released to complete indifference and neglect, or as Zevon himself put it, 'to the sound of one hand clapping'. It quietly and quickly went out of print until Pickwick Records reissued it following the commercial success of *Excitable Boy* in 1978. *Wanted Dead Or Alive* reappeared in 1979, much to its creator's vexation. He made his displeasure known in subsequent interviews, even urging people not to buy it, arguing that it wasn't representative of his current work.

The songwriter hadn't mellowed much regarding his first album when interviewed by Steve Roesser for *Goldmine* in 1995. While conceding that it had 'some amusing things about it', Zevon concluded that the album's most interesting feature was the cover shot, taken by future Industrial Light and Magic special effects cinematographer Richard Edlund.

'Wanted Dead Or Alive' (Kim Fowley, Martin Cerf)

Thanks to a pre-schism gentleman's agreement, it's a Kim Fowley song that opens Zevon's debut album and provides its title. Uncannily, the lyric taps into the singer-songwriter's future predilections for western imagery and the romance of outlaws, anti-heroes and violence. The music is anticipatory too, in a general sense, and specifically for including some semblance of the riff from 1980's *Bad Luck Streak in Dancing School* track 'Jungle Work', though here the rhythm has greater urgency, is driven by Zevon's twelve-string acoustic, and has a seeming Native-Americana-via-Laurel-Canyon pulse. Drummer Drachen Theaker, late of The Crazy World of Arthur Brown, matches Zevon's insistent tempo, while future Byrd Skip Battin's solid bass patterns rein the other two in.

'Wanted Dead Or Alive' may well be the most Zevonian song recorded but not written by Warren, and it serves as a strong opener to his solo debut.

'Hitchhikin' Woman' (Black Ace Turner, Zevon)

Despite many online sources crediting Zevon as the writer of 'Hitchhikin' Woman', it is in fact, a cover of a Black Ace Turner song released in 1960 and given further exposure when covered five years later by producer John Hammond, whom Zevon acknowledged in a 1995 *Goldmine* interview as 'this incredible, overwhelming influence'. While Hammond maintained the spidery death-march pace of the original, Zevon's take is far more sprightly and up-tempo, though quite why this warrants a co-credit is unexplained, particularly since Zevon omits some lyrics and seems to forget others.

The drummer here is Jon Corneal, moonlighting from the Flying Burrito Brothers, and famed rock photographer Ed Caraeff plays maraca. But this is Zevon's show; as well as playing bass, he replaces the original's flat Hawaiian guitar with a blistering burst of harmonica twinned with electric guitar. But there's no escaping the song's origin as a generic blues dirge, and despite the rowdy, spirited shouts of 'Hey!' and 'Ahoo!' throughout – and even a hearty 'Play the blues, boys' delivered with backslapping camaraderie – 'Hitchhikin' Woman' expires some way short of any known excitement threshold. Its only claim to fame is in marking the first appearance on record of Zevon's distinctive velvet growl.

Note: Black Ace Turner's birth name was Babe Lemon Turner, making his adopting a stage name seem somewhat superfluous.

'She Quit Me' (Zevon)

Thanks to Bones Howe's indefatigable efforts, this song found its way onto the soundtrack of future Oscar winner *Midnight Cowboy*, directed by John Schlesinger, and starring Dustin Hoffman and Jon Voight. According to Zevon biographer C. M. Kushins, it was even considered for the main theme (as was 'Lay Lady Lay', but Dylan missed the deadline) before that spot was claimed by Harry Nilsson's version of Fred Neil's 'Everybody's Talkin'.

Singer-songwriter Lesley Miller performed the song in the movie as 'He Quit Me'. Her occasionally histrionic bluesy-soul rendering is superior to Zevon's sparse guitar and harmonica reading. If he was disappointed at someone else doing his song, at least – like Liberace, responding to his critics' claims of vulgarity and lack of talent – he got to cry all the way to the bank; the *Midnight Cowboy* soundtrack earned Zevon his first gold disc, which he gifted to his father.

'Calcutta' (Zevon)

'Calcutta' is more jam-session than song. The six-line lyric is disposed of with undue haste, presumably, so the musicians can *get down*, but what they get down to isn't that interesting. The rhythm section of Skip Battin and

Drachen Theaker are back, but they're very much overpowered by Zevon's rambunctious ivory-tinkling, a hint of organ, and three guitar tracks united only in their discordance. On the plus side, by 2:20, it's all over.

'Iko-Iko' (James Crawford, Barbara Hawkins, Rosa Hawkins, Joan Johnson)

Drachen Theaker's drums are positively reticent here, a surprise considering how percussive the Dixie Cups hit version of the song was. But Zevon and Skip Battin appear to be having a thoroughly enjoyable time, the latter laying down an extraordinarily supple bass line. A backing group called Sweet Trifles make their only recorded appearance, their seeming prime purpose to trade 'Iko' yells with Zevon in a rabble-rousing attempt to add excitement to a song that was never going to shake its novelty status loose.

James Crawford's New Orleans standard has been recorded by a baffling number of artists over the years, but it's a shame Zevon's previously-mentioned 'sudden attack of taste' didn't kick in soon enough to prevent him falling prey to this playground ditty.

'Traveling In The Lightning' (Zevon)

Thus far, *Wanted Dead or Alive* has demonstrated none of the literate lyricism that distinguished Zevon's later work, and that certainly doesn't change here. If anything, this lyric might be the most underwhelming of Zevon's career, the narrator bemoaning travelling from gig to gig in inclement weather, while conveniently omitting any journey made on a sunny day.

It's the album's hardest-rocking number, wherein Zevon does his best Jimi Hendrix impersonation before shifting gear into an effects-laden foray into cosmic country. This description runs the risk of making the song sound more appealing than it is, which is not bad, but not memorable either.

'Tule's Blues' (Zevon)

Tule is Marilyn Livingston, Warren's then-partner and mother of his son Jordan. When she was about to give birth, Warren drove her to the maternity ward, kissed her goodbye and went to the recording studio to work on the album. While there, he noticed an amplifier with the brand name Jordan, and thought that would be a cool name for a kid.

If the above scenario lacks a certain romance, Zevon makes up for it on 'Tule's Blues'. The velvet growl, AWOL since 'Hitchhikin' Woman', is back, but now it's racked with the vulnerability Zevon was never afraid to show in his most soul-searing ballads. Here we begin to see the emergence of that celebrated lyrical prowess:

Oh Tule, it's once I was your knight in golden armour
With the sun behind my hair
My music filled the air with symbols and lightning

As the above stanza illustrates, there's an almost teenage earnestness to 'Tule's Blues' that leaves it dancing dangerously close to sixth-form poetry, but it *is* poetic nonetheless.

It's an unabashed country-rock song, but one that marbles its boisterous shit-kicking core melody with a rich seam of melancholy that buttresses the protagonists' strained relationship: 'It's a sad song we always seem to be singing to each other/You and me, sweet and slightly out of key'. This hoedown-meets-heartbreak continues to the track's end, where the narrator concludes he's trapped in a can't-live-with-her/can't-live-without-her situation:

Oh Tule, it's on account of you that I'll be leaving
'Cross the deep salt sea
Whatever wild worlds I may see
Will be empty without you

It is a neat trick to juxtapose the sad against the celebratory, almost as clever as the phantom fiddle and pedal steel embellishments, despite the sleeve notes crediting only Zevon on guitar, piano, and bass, and a returning Jon Corneal on drums.

'Tule's Blues' is gorgeous, a sparkling early-career diamond-in-the-rough and, quite simply, Warren's first masterpiece. That it's never appeared on any Zevon 'best of' compilation borders on criminal neglect. It should be on them all. It easily holds its own against any later work.

'A Bullet For Ramona' (Paul Evans, Zevon)

This gets a full studio outing here, maintaining the previous track's country-rock. Rhythm section Brent Seawell (bass) and Toxey French (drums) make their sole appearance on the album, with all other instrumentation provided by Zevon. This includes electric guitar and a lovely shuffling acoustic, but he particularly shines on the honky-tonk-style piano filling every available space, and the marxophone, a fretless zither used sparingly in rock music.

Zevon double-tracks his vocal to great effect throughout, as he sings of familiar future themes such as (misplaced) vengeance, violence and the West. It comes as a surprise, therefore, to discover that the lyrics aren't his, but were written by Paul Evans, who had a US hit ten years earlier with novelty song 'Seven Little Girls Sitting In The Back Seat', and enjoyed a top 10 UK hit in 1978 with 'Hello, This is Joannie (The Telephone Answering Machine Song)'.

Eagle-eyed readers may have noticed that Evans received no credit on *The First Sessions* demo version, which presumably is another example of Warren's early practice of neglecting to acknowledge his co-writers.

'Gorilla' (Zevon)

'Gorilla' is the first of several simian songs from Zevon's catalogue, and the second on this album to anticipate 'Jungle Work'. The album's title track may have hinted coyly at that 1980 song, but, appropriately for a song called 'Gorilla', there is no such subtlety here; the riff of the later tune is essentially recycled from the one presented here.

The Battin/Theacker rhythm section is back for its final session, and Zevon once again acts as a one-man band, playing guitars, percussion, marimba and (uncredited) piano. His vocal is buried deep in the mix – mercifully, as 'Gorilla' surely stands as the songwriter's most asinine lyric, as this sample should attest:

Jungle telephone
Ding a dong ding ding
With the red mud
Ching a chong ching ching

Fortunately, this drivel only lasts about a minute. But astonishingly, the track gets worse, as the instrumentation grows more cacophonous, building towards a complete and utter anticlimax.

'Fiery Emblems' (Zevon)
This is an instrumental with no obvious melody. Presumably, its sole purpose is to make the preceding track sound good.

Warren Zevon (1976)

Personnel:
Warren Zevon: vocals, piano, electric piano, harmonica, guitar
Waddy Wachtel: guitar
Bob Glaub: bass
Larry Zack: drums
David Lindley: fiddle, banjo, slide guitar, guitar
Jackson Browne: slide guitar and harmony vocals on 'Backs Turned Looking Down The Path'
Lindsey Buckingham: guitar on 'Backs Turned Looking Down The Path'
Marty David: bass on 'Backs Turned Looking Down The Path'
Gary Mallaber: drums on 'Backs Turned Looking Down The Path' and 'I'll Sleep When I'm Dead'
Bobby Keys: saxophone on 'Poor Poor Pitiful Me', 'Mohammed's Radio' and 'Join Me In L.A.'
Jai Winding: piano on 'Poor Poor Pitiful Me'; organ and synthesizer on 'Join Me In L.A.'
Glenn Frey: rhythm guitar and backing vocals on 'Carmelita'
Strings: The Sid Sharp Strings
Backing vocals: Phil Everly, John David Souther, Jackson Browne, Lindsey Buckingham, Glenn Frey, Don Henley, Stephanie Nicks, Jorge Calderón, Bonnie Raitt, Rosemary Butler, Carl Wilson, Billy Hinsche, Jai Winding, Warren Zevon
Recorded at Sunset Sound and Elektra Sound Recorders, Los Angeles
Producer: Jackson Browne
Release date: 18 May 1976
Label: Asylum
Chart placing: US: 189
Running time: 37:45

Despite *Wanted Dead or Alive*'s spectacular failure, Imperial green-lit a second album. Songs from this period that surfaced after Zevon's death, such as 'Studebaker' and 'The Rosarita Beach Café', show his melodic flair, but apparently, he wanted the project to be an extension of 'Fiery Emblems', the instrumental that closed the previous album. When the Imperial management heard what Zevon was concocting, they decided their association with the singer was done, and cancelled his contract.

In 1971, Zevon landed a gig as keyboard player and musical director for The Everly Brothers, appearing on their unsuccessful comeback album *Stories We Could Tell* the following year. This led to Warren making two important connections; the first being guitarist Waddy Wachtel, who would appear on many future Zevon recordings, and, through him, Crystal Brelsford, who very soon became Waddy's ex-girlfriend.

Warren dumped Tule for Crystal, but because booze was always the third partner in any Zevon relationship, their time together was no less turbulent, and at times was downright scary. In *I'll Sleep When I'm Dead,* Crystal's oral biography of Warren, she tells of the time she discovered Zevon had been hiding liquor in her nine-year-old foster son Bart's outdoor playhouse. A fight ensued, whereupon an enraged and totally hammered Zevon grabbed Bart, got into Crystal's car and drove off, promptly slamming into a trio of parked cars and crashing to a halt in the front window of a house down the street. Zevon was led away in handcuffs, and spent three days in jail. He returned home to a note asking him to leave, but he and Crystal reconciled after he agreed to attend Alcoholics Anonymous. He attended one meeting.

Despite his continuing alcoholism, Warren and Crystal married in Las Vegas in May 1974. Apart from a stint playing the piano in an unsuccessful Don Everly solo tour, not a lot was happening musically for Zevon, a situation that hadn't altered by the time 1975 rolled around. So in spring that year, he and Crystal upped sticks for a new life in Spain. They settled in Sitges – just over 20 miles southwest of Barcelona – and Warren got a job playing in an Irish bar called The Dubliner. It was run by a former mercenary named David Lindell, who enthralled Zevon with his past exploits. They were soon collaborating on a song about a murdered soldier of fortune-seeking vengeance from beyond the grave.

Times were good in Spain, but a couple of items arrived in the mail that brought the couple's sojourn there to a close. The first was a letter from Phil Everly, inviting Warren to arrange and play on his next solo album (Zevon's reggae arrangement of Phil and Don's old hit 'When Will I Be Loved' is more interesting than his sole co-write for the album, a limp ballad called 'January Butterfly'). The second item – which was to make a greater impact – was a postcard from singer-songwriter and all-around Zevon champion Jackson Browne, who exhorted Warren to come home, Browne saying he would secure him a recording contract. Browne proved to be true to his word, and Warren was signed to David Geffen's Asylum Records, home of West Coast wunderkinds like Browne, Linda Ronstadt, Joni Mitchell and The Eagles.

There was a lot riding on *Warren Zevon.* Jackson Browne practically begged Asylum owner David Geffen to sign his friend, and the steadfastly-unconvinced label owner only agreed on the condition that Browne himself produce the album. In this capacity, Browne set about structuring the record to serve as the world's introduction to a major songwriting talent, purposely casting aside lighthearted-if-macabre future fan-favourites like 'Excitable Boy' and 'Werewolves Of London', in favour of tracks he felt best represented Zevon's literary bent. By adding an Everly Brother and a Beach Boy, he populated the record with rock royalty, and crammed it with the cream of California rock, with various Eagles, Fleetwood Mac members, and Browne himself all contributing. The so-called Mellow Mafia would iron out Zevon's rough spots, making the album more palatable to the public and the airwaves. But despite Browne's best efforts, *Warren Zevon* sold only 80,000 copies on its initial release, and limped to number 189. For all its big star-studded budget, it was only slightly more wanted than *Wanted Dead Or Alive.*

But what the album lacked in commercial kudos, it made up for in critical acclaim. *The Village Voice*'s Paul Nelson was the most succinct: 'I'll come right out and say it: Warren Zevon is a major artist'. Stephen Holden of *Rolling Stone* thought the album to be 'a very auspicious accomplishment', while, in the *New York Times*, Kit Rachlis called Zevon 'a champion contender who's only completed his first round'.

Apart from being essentially a *debut* album from a relatively unknown performer, perhaps *Warren Zevon* faltered because its creator, while being part of the West Coast scene, was also quite apart from it. Even the album cover – a slightly blurred nighttime shot of a bespectacled Warren wearing a suit, a dress code he would adopt on all his Asylum covers – distinguished him from the double denim of his labelmates. The often-dark subject matter, twisted cynicism, jet-black humour and classical training also marked him as atypical from other Asylum artists, with the obvious exception of Beat Street hobo Tom Waits. *Newsweek* reviewer Janet Maslin agreed, calling Zevon 'that refreshing rarity: a pop singer with comic detachment ... out to demolish every cliché in the Asylum bin'.

Warren Zevon has stood the test of time, with many critics regarding it as his finest album, a conclusion one can easily understand. Songs as strong as 'Desperados Under The Eaves' and 'The French Inhaler' mean that the album inevitably has to have lesser songs, but there's no filler. Anyone curious about Zevon could do worse than starting here.

'Frank And Jessie James' (Zevon)
Frank and Jesse James were ruthless killers, both of whom took part in the 1864 Centralia massacre in which 24 unarmed Union soldiers were scalped and mutilated. Frank also participated in the previous year's raid on Lawrence, Kansas, that left 160 to 190 of the town's men and boys dead. Yet despite the James' abhorrent deeds and murderous reputations, they have been transformed into folk heroes, thanks initially to the efforts of newspaperman John Newman Edwards, a former Confederate officer who glorified the two brothers in their lifetime, hoping it would re-instil pride in ex-Confederates. It was Edwards who first compared the brothers to Robin Hood, and while the James Gang did indeed rob from the rich, there is not a shred of historical evidence that suggests they ever gave to the poor. After Jesse James' 1882 murder, dime novels continued this romanticisation, with radio serials, movies and television shows carrying the tradition into the 20th century (The fact that Jesse James Jnr. played his father in his first two film depictions, strongly suggests historical accuracy ended up on the cutting room floor). But no medium perpetuated this myth more than music, beginning with the much-covered 19th-century folk song 'Jesse James', and continuing here on the opening song of Warren Zevon's major-label debut.

The chorus encourages the James brothers to 'Keep on riding, riding, riding/'Til you clear your names', as if their crimes were some misunderstanding *a la* the American television western *Alias Smith and Jones*, while the last verse assures the listener that, 'the poor Missouri farmers knew/Frank and Jesse do the best they could'.

Mythologising aside, Zevon is biographically correct and even went to his local library to ensure he had his facts right. Thus, they did indeed join up with Quantrill when 'war broke out between the states', and 'After Appomattox, they *were* on the losing side'.

Written during his time with the Everly Brothers, Zevon stated the song was 'for and about' Phil and Don, though this is in no way obvious from the lyric. Perhaps the songwriter was metaphorically comparing the Everly's failure to adapt to change in popular music to the James brothers' inability to fit into a post-Civil War world. The Everly Brothers never recorded the song, but Phil Everly supplies the vocal harmony here.

Musically, the song's faux-folksiness and historical setting are evoked in terms of general melody and, especially, David Lindley's middle-eight fiddle embellishments, with Zevon's uncredited harmonica playing also setting the scene. The song also appears to be on nodding terms with Aaron Copland's 'Rodeo'. Despite the *aw shucks* elements, the music is also something of a widescreen epic, and would not have been out of place on the soundtrack of *The Long Riders*, Walter Hill's 1980 western about the James-Younger gang.

'Mama Couldn't Be Persuaded' (Zevon)

This is a jaunty mid-paced rock and roller that also indulges in some mythologising, this time about Warren's parents' marriage, which, it will be remembered, was less than successful. The lyrics primarily centre on Zevon's maternal grandparents pleading 'with their daughter/Don't marry that gamblin' man', while the daughter, in turn 'was determined that she wanted Bill' (Stumpy Zevon's first name being William). In art as in life, the 'Gambler tried to be a family man/Though it didn't suit his style'. The whole tale is told in frolicking good humour, exhibiting none of Zevon's celebrated black comedy, and which belies the extremely turbulent relationship William (and by extension, Warren) had with his wife and her parents. The song is too lightweight and frothy, rendering it as the album's weakest track, but it does act as a foil to some of the dark paths later songs will travel.

'Backs Turned Looking Down The Path' (Zevon)

Bass, supported by some laid-back drums, introduces a song that, according to Crystal Zevon, Warren claimed several times over the years to be his best. It would be nice to know why he thought this, but one suspects he would be alone in that belief. Not that there is anything wrong with the song; it has a silky late-night groove, with Lindsey Buckingham playing acoustic so delicately, his guitar could be strung with cobwebs, while Jackson Browne contributes slide and vocal harmonies equally as gossamer-light. To quote the Small Faces, 'It's all too beautiful', but the skills of the players are too exquisite for a song that never threatens to rise above pleasant, and while 'Frank And Jesse James' demonstrated that the engine was on lyrically, here the wheels are just spinning in the mud.

'Hasten Down The Wind' (Zevon)

This is the second song in the 'Tule Trilogy' that started with 'Tule's Blues' from *Wanted Dead or Alive*. The lyrics deal with a relationship at the end of its road, as the narrator realises he no longer recognises the woman he fell in love with, in turn acknowledging 'She thinks she needs to be free'. Despite some uncertainty on both parts, the narrator acquiesces, bidding her to 'Hasten down the wind'.

The title's 'down the wind' (more commonly 'whistle down the wind') originates from falconry, meaning to cast someone or something off to its own fate, or, simply, to let go. Shakespeare uses it in *Othello*. When the title character finds out his wife Desdemona has been unfaithful, he says, 'I'll whistle her off and let her down the wind, to pray at fortune'.

It's a tender ballad, with lovely, understated playing, especially from Bob Glaub (bass) and Larry Zack (drums), the rhythm section on the bulk of the album. David Lindley supplies splendidly mournful slide guitar, and Phil Everly returns with quietly spellbinding vocal harmonies. The Sid Sharp Strings, who had previously worked with Glen Campbell, the Beach Boys, Neil Diamond, and many others, make their first of many appearances on Zevon songs.

Linda Ronstadt's cover version of the song provided the title for her platinum-selling 1976 album *Hasten Down the Wind*; Waddy Wachtel played lead guitar on both versions.

'Poor Poor Pitiful Me' (Zevon)

According to Zevon, this rocker in touch with its country-and-western side was inspired by Desmond Dekker and The Aces' 1969 hit 'Israelites'. This influence is not easy to discern, save perhaps for the lyric's woe-is-me nature. Otherwise, there is scarce comparison between Dekker's ode to surviving grinding poverty in Jamaica and Zevon's botherations over ill-planned suicide attempts and fetishist tendencies, ludicrous scenarios apparently conceived as a friendly riposte to (and parody of) Jackson Browne's more depressing songs.

The regular band of Wachtel, Lindley, Glaub and Zack are joined by long-time Rolling Stones saxophonist Bobby Keys. Lindsey Buckingham provides enthusiastic backing vocals, and everyone sounds like they are having a hoot. The song became a concert staple for the rest of Zevon's career.

Linda Ronstadt again proved to be a stalwart champion of Zevon's music, covering 'Poor Poor Pitiful Me' on 1977's *Simple Dreams*, her biggest-selling album. Released as a single in January 1978, it reached 31 in the US. Deciding she wasn't that kind of girl, Ronstadt ditched the sadomasochistic last verse in favour of a previously dropped earlier verse from Zevon's original.

'The French Inhaler' (Zevon)

Despite a deceptive sprightly piano intro that wouldn't sound out of place in the court of Mozart patron Hieronymus von Colloredo, this song is Zevon at his most caustic:

How're you going to get around
In this sleazy bedroom town
If you don't put yourself up for sale?

Or how about:

Drugs and wine and flattering light
You must try it again till you get it right

No one is going to accuse Zevon of being a silver-tongued devil based on these, but he saves his most savage swipe for last:

And when the lights came up at two
I caught a glimpse of you
And your face looked like something
Death brought with him in his suitcase

The subject of these spiteful attacks was Marilyn 'Tule' Livingston, Zevon's former partner and mother of his son Jordan. It's a post-breakup rather than breakup song, Warren angry that Livingston went on to see another musician. In 2005, on the official Warren Zevon website, Jordan Zevon stated that the words of 'The French Inhaler' were 'my favourite lyrics that Dad ever wrote. The ultimate FU/breakup song ... Of course, it sucks that my Mom was the recipient of the above-mentioned FU, but still, as a songwriter, you've gotta love it'. In a 2013 *Guardian* interview, Jordan even remembers his mother being a fan of the song: 'Despite the subject matter, my mom would play that song to me after a couple of glasses of wine, and laugh and say, "Isn't that brilliant?"'.

The song has a puzzling postscript:

The French Inhaler
He stamped and mailed her
'So long, Norman' she said
'So long, Norman'

The 'Norman' and 'mailed her' appear to be a not-so-subtle reference to American writer Norman Mailer, who'd recently published a controversial biography about another Marilyn, Marilyn Monroe. Why he appears at the end of such a personal song is unknown, but Jordan Zevon confirmed on the Zevon website that Norman Mailer was indeed the line's subject, cryptically prefacing it by saying, 'I can't tell you the specific reason why'.

Guitarist Waddy Watchtel knows he's not the star here, so he's never flashy, but his dedication to serving the songs is evident throughout the album, and especially on 'The French Inhaler', his clever fretwork lighting up what is ostensibly a piano-led song. Eagles Glenn Frey and Don Henley deliver angelic harmonies that seem out of place amidst the slightly seedy ambience. The result is a bitter, twisted masterpiece, but a masterpiece nonetheless.

For the record, French inhaling is when a smoker exhales from the mouth while simultaneously inhaling through the nose, causing a steady stream of smoke to flow from mouth to nose.

'Mohammed's Radio' (Zevon)

This is a paean to music's power to momentarily free the listener from the frustrations and disappointments of everyday life. The plaintive verses relate the drudgery – 'Everybody's desperate, trying to make ends meet' – before Lindsey Buckingham and, especially, Stevie Nicks' harmonies send the chorus soaring into something deliriously 'sweet and soulful', transforming the song from rock and roll to gospel. Bobby Keys' wistful saxophone serves as the bridge between the humdrum and the hymnal.

Drummer Eddie Ponder is quoted in Crystal Zevon's biography as saying this song title was inspired by something he and Warren glimpsed while on Don Everly's 1974 solo tour. It was the end of October when they stopped in Aspen, Colorado. Watching a Halloween parade, Zevon spotted a man with a learning disability, dressed as a sheikh, walking by with a transistor radio pressed to his ear. Warren then coined the title 'Mohammed's Radio', two words he felt sat nicely together, inspiring him to work it up into a fully-fledged song.

This was the fourth and final song Linda Ronstadt covered from this album, this time on her double-platinum 1978 long-player *Living in the USA*, her third and final US chart-topper. Considering Zevon's major label debut only reached 189, it is possible he earned more from the four Ronstadt covers than he did from this or any of his solo efforts.

'I'll Sleep When I'm Dead' (Zevon)

A sparse, sloping, chugging rocker that lurches into existence via a fade-in eschews a traditional chorus in favour of Zevon and Jorge Calderón's animated background conversation, during which Zevon flails on harmonica and drummer Gary Mallaber discovers his cymbals. Jackson Browne displays his production chops by sequencing 'I'll Sleep When I'm Dead' between the gentler 'Mohammed's Radio' and darker 'Carmelita', keeping the album interesting and lightening the mood. After five four-line verses and a final burst of harmonica, the song careens into its fade-out. It's a fun, if slightly throwaway track.

Arguably the song's main significance is the debut appearance of Jorge Calderón, who formed a lifelong friendship with Zevon, playing on all his

29

studio albums except 2002's *My Ride's Here*. Zevon met Calderón when Crystal enlisted his aid in bailing Warren out of the drunk tank.

This song title also served as the title of Crystal's 2007 warts and all biography of her former husband.

'Carmelita' (Zevon)

'Carmelita' is a junkie's lament, the howl of a lost soul, an attempt to out-depress Lou Reed's *Berlin* in one song, and a short story compressed into three verses and a chorus. Like any good storyteller, Zevon sets the scene with a wonderfully atmospheric opening: 'I hear mariachi static on my radio/And the tubes they glow in the dark'. That faint blueish-white glimmer is the song's only light, however, and darkness is encircling.

The verses paint a grim picture. The narrator is no longer receiving methadone to deal with his addiction, and 'They' have cut off his girlfriend Carmelita's welfare cheque. As a result, he's 'sittin' here playing solitaire/With my pearl-handled deck'. The final verse (presumably a flashback) relates the selling of the narrator's last and most-prized possession, his Smith Corona typewriter, to buy drugs 'down on Alvarado Street/By the Pioneer Chicken stand'. Like many Angelenos, our chronicler had dreams – in this case, of being a writer – but his addiction has laid them to rest. This verse recalls the scene in Charles Jackson's novel *The Lost Weekend* (1944), where the main character Don Birnam attempts to sell his typewriter to buy booze. Billy Wilder adapted the novel for the big screen the following year, and it's no stretch to imagine Zevon being familiar with both.

In the chorus, the narrator calls out to Carmelita to hold him tighter as he feels he's 'sinking down', but the first verse had already informed the listener that he is alone in Echo Park, Los Angeles, while she is in Ensenada, Mexico. There is no one to offer succour in his hour of darkness.

Despite the pitch-black subject matter, the track has an airiness, thanks to the delicate Spanish guitar throughout, which links pleasingly to the opening line's mariachi reference. The credits list Waddy Wachtel, Glenn Frey and David Lindley as the guitarists, but alas don't distinguish who was the prime Spanish finger-picker.

The first-released version of 'Carmelita' was by folk singer Murray McLauchlin on his self-titled second album in 1972, predating Zevon's take by four years. The big difference between the two is that McLauchlin sounds like he's singing a song, whereas the guy who wrote it sounds like he's living it. In addition to McLauchlin and the inevitable La Ronstadt, 'Carmelita' has been covered by a range of artists, including Flaco Jiminez (featuring Dwight Yoakam), GG Allin, Willy DeVille, The Bronx and The Wildhearts.

'Join Me In L.A.' (Zevon)

This is a skeletal but satisfying slice of after-midnight funk. There's no story, just a series of vignettes, the most intriguing being the opening couplet: 'Well, they say this place is evil/That ain't why I stay'. Ned Doheny replaces Waddy Wachtel on guitar, gently sparring with Bobby Keys' saxophone after each verse. But it's the irresistible siren call of Bonnie Raitt and Rosemary Butler's backing vocals that sell the song. With the titular invitation positively oozing with wicked promise, who *wouldn't* want to join them in L.A.?

'Desperados Under The Eaves' (Zevon)

The song begins with the Sid Sharp Strings revisiting the piano motif that kick-started 'Frank and Jesse James', before Waddy Wachtel's world-weary guitar provides a bridge to the song proper. 'I was sitting in the Hollywood Hawaiian Hotel', sings Warren about one of his former residences. It sounds lovely, but in the sleeve notes to the posthumous release *Preludes: Rare and Unreleased Recordings*, Crystal Zevon notes that Zevon stayed in the Hollywood Hawaiian 'during a low period in the late '60s' when 'Warren was living from motel to motel' and 'couldn't afford The Tropicana anymore. He spent several weeks stepping over the junkies who blocked his doorway, and sharing stories with the winos camped out on the corner of Yucca and Gower'. Maybe not so idyllic then. If 'Carmelita' was a junkie's lament, 'Desperados Under The Eaves' is the song of the unrepentant alcoholic on a mission to drink 'all the salty margaritas in Los Angeles'; the croak in the voice suggests he won't stop there.

The narrator laments the detritus of his life, being unable to pay his bill, unable to find a girl that understands him, before concluding that even the sun looks angry at him. He notices the hum of the air conditioner, and joins in, words no longer necessary, and it's here that the despondency littering the song metamorphoses into something altogether more hopeful, as Carl Wilson, Billy Hinsche, Jai Winding and Jackson Browne join Zevon in valiantly trying to match Sid Sharp's gloriously lush and uplifting orchestration, surely a highlight in that veteran arranger's career. The narrator's initial despair becomes a soaring battle hymn of the downtrodden, and the simple line 'Look away down Gower Avenue, look away' takes the twilight Los Angeles the album inhabits and transforms it into something every bit as romantic as the New Jersey of Bruce Springsteen's 'Born To Run' and 'Thunder Road'.

'Desperados Under The Eaves' pips 'The French Inhaler' as the album's best track, and it remains one of Zevon's absolute finest, arguably his best. In 2014, *LA Weekly* placed 'Desperados Under The Eaves' in their 20 Best Songs Written About L.A. list, and Bob Dylan referenced the song in his 2020 epic 'Murder Most Foul'.

As for the Hollywood Hawaiian Hotel? Zevon really *couldn't* pay his bill, so fled in the night, aided and abetted by David Marks. Upon finding a degree of fame years later, Zevon returned to pay his debt, but the hotel asked for signed copies of *Warren Zevon* instead. Prior to all this, the hotel had another starring role in rock and roll lore, as it was from there that Fleetwood Mac guitarist Jeremy Spencer popped out to buy cigarettes, and never came back, having joined religious organisation The Children of God.

The Hollywood Hawaiian is gone now, with several online sources claiming it is now the Princess Grace Apartments, while Jordan Zevon says it's a mall. Who is right? It doesn't really matter. Like the original Pioneer Chicken stand, it now exists only in the legendary landscape of Warren Zevon's Los Angeles.

Excitable Boy (1978)

Personnel:
Warren Zevon: vocals, piano, organ, synthesizer
Waddy Wachtel: guitar, synthesizer
Leland Sklar, Kenny Edwards: bass
Russell Kunkel, Rick Morotta: drums
John McVie: bass on 'Werewolves Of London'
Mick Fleetwood: drums on 'Werewolves Of London'
Danny Kortchmar: percussion on 'Johnny Strikes Up The Band'; guitar on 'Nighttime In The Switching Yard'
Jeff Porcaro: drums, percussion on 'Nighttime In The Switching Yard'
Jim Horn: saxophone, recorders
Greg Ladanyi: bell on 'Nighttime In The Switching Yard'
Arthur Gerst: Mexican harp on 'Veracruz'
Luis Damian: jarana on 'Veracruz'
Manuel Vesquez: requinto jarocho on 'Veracruz'
Jorge Calderón: Spanish vocal on 'Veracruz'
Backing vocals: Waddy Wachtel, Jackson Browne, Kenny Edwards, Jorge Calderón, John David Souther, Linda Ronstadt, Jennifer Warnes, Karla Bonoff, Warren Zevon
Producers: Jackson Browne, Waddy Wachtel
Recorded at The Sound Factory, Los Angeles
Release date: 18 January 1978
Label: Asylum
Chart placing: US: 8
Running time: 31.29

Warren Zevon had been well-received, but its sales were strictly chump change compared to records his Asylum labelmates released in 1976. Linda Ronstadt's *Hasten Down the Wind* was a Grammy-winning, platinum seller, reaching number 3 and topping the country chart. Jackson Browne's *The Pretender* peaked at 5, spent 35 weeks on the chart and eventually went triple-platinum. Meanwhile, The Eagles' *Hotel California* topped the chart for an astonishing 130 weeks, ultimately selling 32,000,000 copies worldwide. Even Asylum's other oddball, Tom Waits, reached 89 with *Small Change*, a full one hundred places higher than Zevon's effort. The pressure was on for a second Zevon album that would show a marked improvement in sales.

But there were a couple of sizeable barriers to Zevon achieving this goal, the first being that he was a chronic alcoholic and coke fiend. Zevon was an admirer of writers Ernest Hemingway and F. Scott Fitzgerald, and bought into their belief about substance abuse being a well of creativity. The second stumbling block was that Zevon had been nursing the songs on his Asylum debut for years, and that well was now pretty much depleted. All he had were quirky co-writes, songs about werewolves, seductive psycho-killers and ghostly guns-for-hire. None of them had made the cut for the first album,

33

and, in a musical landscape being terraformed by the dual onslaught of disco and new wave, none of them screamed *hit*.

Jackson Browne was again the producer, but he had his doubts. The previous album's lack of success, and the complete failure of its two singles, 'Hasten Down The Wind' and 'I'll Sleep When I'm Dead', had shaken Browne's faith in his own judgement. He now found himself reconsidering the unconventional numbers he'd banished from the first album. Their friendship notwithstanding, he also had problems with Zevon himself, whose idiosyncrasies and permanent drunkenness could be confrontational and exhausting. Last, but far from least, Browne had his own demons to wrestle with. Phyllis Major, his wife of just a few months and mother of his son Ethan, committed suicide in March 1976, an action that understandably left Browne devastated. To cope, he listened to the counsel of friends recommending he lose himself in his work, so he dutifully finished recording *The Pretender* album and then toured. But the well-intentioned advice hadn't taken. Browne hadn't had time to grieve and come to terms with his wife's death, let alone begin the recovery process, so probably the last thing he needed was studio time with his most volatile friend. His solution was to enlist guitarist Waddy Wachtel as co-producer and chief lion tamer.

Excitable Boy is a classic, equal in quality to its predecessor, and another ideal introduction to the artist. Though it's a couple of songs short of the debut, it benefits from superior production, and introduces the political-history song that would feature on and off in Zevon's work from here on. The two examples here – 'Roland the Headless Thompson Gunner' and 'Veracruz' – showcase a songwriter at the top of his game. At the other end of the spectrum is 'Accidentally Like A Martyr', a heartbreaker that forges the template and sets the bar for Zevon's future ballads. Meanwhile, there are the straight-outta-Bedlam songs, signposted by the previous album's 'I'll Sleep When I'm Dead', but here arriving fully formed courtesy of 'Werewolves Of London', 'Lawyers, Guns And Money' and the title track. The only chink in the armour is the oddball 'Nighttime In The Switching Yard'.

Critics loved the album. Barbara Charone of *Sounds* called it 'the best. No thesaurus could provide sufficient adjectives'. Geoffrey Himes of *The Unicorn Times* said the album 'marks (the) emergence of a major songwriter'. That otherness that separated Zevon from his peers was recognised. Robert Christgau in the *Village Voice*: 'The further these songs get from Ronstadtland, the more I like them'.

In terms of sales, *Excitable Boy* was in fact, the closest Zevon ever got to 'Ronstadtland'. Buoyed by the previous album's critical acclaim, the success of 'Werewolves Of London' and – it should be acknowledged – the musical patronage of Linda Ronstadt, *Excitable Boy* was a bonafide hit, reaching eight on the *Billboard* album chart and earning Warren Zevon his first gold record as a solo artist.

'Johnny Strikes Up the Band' (Zevon)

With that title, this song *had* to open *Excitable Boy*, and fortunately, the song is worthy of pole position. Zevon on piano, Wachtel on guitar, and prolific session-bassist Leland Sklar provide a shimmering, dreamy introduction, brought rudely to attention by the snare drum of the equally prolific Russell Kunkel, in turn ushering in Zevon's velvet growl. His distinctive voice is deeper and warmer than two years previously, the unexpected and only pleasant consequence of his industrial-level cigarette and alcohol consumption.

The track is a mid-tempo rocker, with a lovely guitar solo that could've been given more space to develop. Zevon plays descending scales behind Wachtel's guitar, before Kunkel ends the middle section with a repeat of the snare that kicked the song off. The final verse then unfolds, leaving a reprise of the soothing introduction.

Various internet commentators have suggested who inspired the titular Johnny, with John Lennon, John Lydon (then Johnny Rotten) and Johnny Carson all named as suspects. This last named allows the more inventive lyric detective to throw in long-time Carson producer Fred de Cordova as the 'Freddie' that appears in the song. The following lines have naturally led others to conclude that Johnny is a drug dealer:

And Johnny is my main man
He's the keeper of the keys
He'll put your mind at ease
He's guaranteed to please

But what almost everyone agrees on, is that this song – like the previous album's 'Mohammed's Radio' – is a celebration of the redemptive and restorative power of music, specifically rock and roll.

Zevon admitted to borrowing the title from Ernst Krenek's German Weimer-era opera *Jonny Spielt Auf* (*Johnny Strikes Up*), while, according to biographer C. M. Kushins, Zevon based Freddie on the then-recently-deceased blues guitarist Freddie King. It's equally feasible that Freddie's presence can be explained away by the fact he rhymes with 'ready' and 'steady'.

'Roland The Headless Thompson Gunner' (David Lindell, Zevon)

In the late-1970s, it wasn't uncommon for the music press to refer to Warren Zevon as 'The Sam Peckinpah of Rock', a phrase first coined by Paul Nelson in *Rolling Stone*. This is the song that most earns him that sobriquet.

A gothic, geo-political ghost story and an updating of Washington Irving's *The Legend of Sleepy Hollow* for the post-Vietnam era, 'Roland' tells of a Norwegian soldier of fortune risen from the grave to avenge his murder at the hands of Van Owen, a former colleague. After achieving retribution, Roland continues to haunt the world's trouble spots 'In Ireland, in Lebanon/In Palestine and Berkeley'. This last-named was presumably a nod to Berkeley, California, a hotbed of protest in the late-1960s, most notoriously when the occupation of People's Park resulted in multiple incidents of violence and police brutality.

The lyric name-checks Patty Hearst, granddaughter of publishing magnate William Randolph Hearst, who shot to international notoriety in 1974 when she was kidnapped by left-wing terrorist group the Symbionese Liberation Army. She was later accused of committing crimes as an alleged member of the SLA, and served time before President Jimmy Carter commuted her sentence. She crops up in the song's ambiguous closing lyric, 'Patty Hearst/Heard the burst of Roland's Thompson gun/And bought it'. At face value, it could mean that Hearst, through family or SLA connections, came into possession of Roland's gun. Alternatively, and more appealing considering Zevon's dark humour, it means that the hapless Hearst has fallen victim to the grisly gunslinger, 'buying it' being an idiom for being killed. If the latter, then Zevon was bending reality every bit as audaciously as Quentin Tarantino would later do in *Inglourious Basterds* and *Once Upon a Time in Hollywood*: as, as of this writing, the real Patty Hearst is very much alive.

Historical accuracy seemed less important in this song than it did in, for example, 'Frank And Jesse James'. In the opening verse, Roland sets off for Biafra, which means he participated in the Nigerian Civil War, *not* the 'Congo war' as stated in verse two. This being the case, he would've been fighting the Igbo people and *not* the Bantu as the lyric says.

Returning briefly to Hollywood, 'Roland' is paid unlikely homage in the 1997 film *The Lost World: Jurassic Park*. Pete Postlethwaite plays big game hunter Roland Tembo, and Vince Vaughn plays documentarian Nick Van Owen, neither of whom appeared in the original Michael Crichton novels but were introduced by screenwriter David Koepp and named after the characters in this song. Zevon possibly lifted *his* protagonist's name from *The Song of Roland*, an epic poem from 11th-century France. 'Roland The Headless Thompson Gunner' might not be as long, but it *is* an epic, a four-minute movie with a matching Homeric soundtrack, but one that knows act two is a tragedy.

It begins with Zevon alone at the piano, playing an air that is vaguely martial and reminiscent of 'When Johnny Comes Marching Home'. Russell Kunkel joins for the first verse, simply keeping time with the bass drum, while Zevon adds a slight strain of melancholy to his playing, anticipating Roland's murder in verse three. Waddy Wachtel and Bob Glaub join on guitar and bass respectively, Glaub instantly reprising the excellence he brought to *Warren Zevon*. Zevon foregoes his oft-romanticised violence for grim realism: Roland and comrades fight 'knee-deep in gore'.

After Van Owen kills Roland at the behest of the CIA, the Gentleman Boys (Browne, Wachtel, J. D. Souther, Kenny Edwards and Jorge Calderón) provide a Greek chorus descant, informing the listener that 'time stands still for Roland / 'Til he evens up the score'. More significantly, Zevon introduces a spectral organ sound that signifies a ghostly presence, while Kunkel brings in a military drum roll as Roland hunts down and promptly dispatches the man that murdered him. Once again, the violence is brutal: Roland doesn't utter a word when he confronts Van Owen (although this might have more to do with lacking a head than simply being tight-lipped), but doesn't stop shooting until he blows Van Owen's body from Mombasa to Johannesburg. The eerie keyboard returns as Roland is 'still wandering through the night', visiting the hot spots mentioned above before his encounter with Patti Hearst, wherein Zevon and Kunkel combine to recreate the ratta-tat-tat of Roland's Thompson gun.

This song is a perfect example of storytelling through words and music, and if I was trying to sell Warren Zevon in one song, it would be this one. It was the last song he ever performed publicly, at the end of the 30 October 2002 edition of *The Late Show with David Letterman*.

'Excitable Boy' (LeRoy P. Marinell, Zevon)

After the mayhem of the last three minutes and forty-five seconds, the title track's upbeat Scott-Joplin-like piano opening promises some light relief, and 'Yakety Yak' sax styling and doo-wop backing vocals all add to the fun. But don't be fooled; 'Excitable Boy' is part two of what Zevon biographer George Plasketes referred to as this album's 'terror trilogy'.

As lyrically playful as it is musically, 'Excitable Boy' could be an off-the-cuff Alice Cooper/Randy Newman co-write. The track remains lively throughout, but the words turn decidedly deadly, as the character quickly moves far beyond anyone's definition of mere excitability. Verse one establishes his highly-strung credentials, when he rubs a hot pot-roast all over his chest. He soon progresses to physically abusing cinema employees, eventually raping and killing the girl he invites to the Junior Prom (In a likely nod to Zevon's former employers The Everly Brothers, the victim is referred to as 'little Susie'.) As if that's not horrific enough, he takes her home, presumably fulfilling a pre-Prom promise to her parents. After ten years' of incarceration, he digs up her remains and makes a cage from her bones.

Is 'Excitable Boy' a slab of sick humour? Or is it perhaps a comment on how desensitised to violence we have become? Or, as Geoffrey Himes wrote in *The Unicorn Times*, is it 'actually a bitter parody of those that excuse rape with "He's just an excitable boy"'? Who knows, but while it may have been accepted as an amusing little ditty back in 1978 (apart from, reportedly, Joni Mitchell), it is difficult to see its casual and graphic violence towards women passing without comment in the Me Too-era, even if it is satirical.

In interviews around the album's release, Zevon proudly revealed that verse one was autobiographical and that he did indeed once smear a pot-roast all over his chest. What is startling is that none of his interlocutors found that behaviour odd enough to ask why.

'Werewolves Of London' (Marinell, Waddy Wachtel, Zevon)

Phil Everly was watching the 1935 horror movie *Werewolf of London*, which naturally inspired him to ask Zevon to write a dance song called 'Werewolves Of London' for Everly's new solo album. In the end, those lyrical lycanthropes never darkened Everly's door, becoming instead Zevon's signature song, the one that people know, even if they don't know who Warren Zevon is. It reached 21 in the US and was a top-20 hit in Canada, New Zealand and Australia. It only reached 87 in the UK, though that placing is disproportionate with the airplay it received.

The rollicking piano riff and chord progression are redolent of Lynyrd Skynyrd's 'Sweet Home Alabama', a similarity Kid Rock successfully exploited when he mashed the two on his 2008 single 'All Summer Long'.

'Werewolves Of London' is the third in Plasketes' terror trilogy, and like 'Excitable Boy', the brisk, lively melody partially offsets the lyric's lurking menace. In Plasketes' biography *Warren Zevon: Desperado of Los Angeles*, Jackson Browne saw the song's werewolf as a metaphor for 'a really well-dressed ladies' man ... a gigolo thing', but that makes lines like 'You better stay away from him/He'll rip your lungs out, Jim' difficult to interpret. Perhaps sometimes a song about a werewolf is simply a song about a werewolf.

> I saw a werewolf with a Chinese menu in his hand
> Walking through the streets of Soho in the rain
> He was looking for the place called Lee Ho Fook's
> Gonna get a big dish of beef chow mein

In 2004, BBC Radio 2 listeners voted these the best opening line (sic) in a song, beating off competition from Bill Haley, Jimi Hendrix, Bruce Springsteen and Lynyrd Skynyrd. But, though unproclaimed by listeners everywhere, surely the song's line 'Little old lady got mutilated late last night' is the best use of alliteration in a pop song.

Zevon wrote some truly magnificent songs, but did it ever irk him that this novelty number was his best-known composition? He told Steven P. Wheeler in a 1990 *Happening* interview: 'It didn't become an albatross. It's better that I bring something to mind than nothing. There are times when I prefer that it was 'Bridge Over Troubled Water', but I don't think bad about the song'.

The eatery named in the song, Lee Ho Fook, was a real establishment, the first Chinese restaurant in the UK to receive a Michelin star. It proudly advertised the Zevon connection in its window until its 2008 closure. I visited the restaurant three years earlier, and anyone reading this book can probably guess what I ordered.

'Accidentally Like A Martyr' (Zevon)

Quirky, dark, intelligent, humorous, and, most especially, literate; all words commonly used to describe Zevon's songwriting. But 'romantic' should also be on the list because he was the author of many beautiful, often desperate romantic ballads.

There had been hints of this on the previous album ('Hasten Down The Wind' for example), but 'Accidentally Like A Martyr', one of only three solo-written songs on this platter, is arguably Zevon's first great ballad. The language alone is exquisite, the title as hopelessly starry-eyed as it is meaningless. Who wouldn't want to make the 'mad love/Shadow love/Random love and abandoned love' of the chorus? It all sounds decidedly exciting and just a tad risqué.

The rhythm section of Leland Sklar and Russell Kunkel demonstrate again why they were never short of work, as they anchor Zevon's feather-light piano-playing and Wachtel's keening slide guitar, each of which perform a delicate ostinato in the instrumental middle section and at the end.

The song was a particular favourite of Bob Dylan. He titled his 1997 album *Time Out of Mind* after a line in the song, and after Zevon announced his terminal illness, Dylan performed it live 22 times in 2002. A cover of it crops up on American rock band The War On Drugs' 2020 *Live Drugs* album, with frontman Adam Granduciel sounding very Dylanesque.

'Nighttime In The Switching Yard' (Jorge Calderón, Lindell, Wachtel, Zevon)

Rock acts doing disco was a thing in the late 1970s. The Bee Gees were the obvious pioneers, their 1975 album *Main Course* veering towards funk and away from the pop of their previous albums. With the release of the *Saturday Night Fever* soundtrack two years later, they sailed deep into mirrorball territory and enjoyed their greatest success. Other English acts followed, including The Rolling Stones with 'Miss You', Rod Stewart with 'Do Ya Think I'm Sexy', and even – bizarrely – a smattering of songs on the 1980 Gentle Giant album *Civilian*. Americans getting in on the act included artists as diverse as Blondie, Kiss, Dr. Hook, Sparks, and Frank Zappa.

'Nighttime In The Switching Yard' was Zevon's entry into the genre, a song that was gloriously untroubled by the 'literate' tag, but one that was groove focused, inherently danceable, and undeniably D-I-S-C-O. Asylum thought it could be a contender in the singles chart and released it as the follow up to 'Werewolves Of London', but it stiffed spectacularly. Musically, it's merely okay, maybe even within shouting distance of some of his contemporaries' floor-filling efforts, but someone should've twigged sooner that a song about trainspotting was never going to be much of an excitement generator. Moreover, because it's a track for moving to rather than listening to, its placement between 'Accidentally Like A Martyr' and 'Veracruz' is aurally jarring.

David Lindell was given a songwriting credit because he apparently entertained Warren with stories about men who manually changed rail tracks, and Zevon bafflingly found this interesting enough to share with Calderón (a surefire setup for *Wayne's World*'s Wayne and Garth to proclaim their unworthiness if ever there was one). Lindell's credit demonstrates a generosity on Zevon's part that is markedly different from the lyme and cybelle days when collaborators could find their names MIA.

'Veracruz' (Calderón, Zevon)

Inspired by a television documentary on Mexican revolutionary Emiliano Zapata, but centring on the United States attack on Veracruz in April 1914, this was Zevon's first co-write with Jorgé Calderón, who was to become Zevon's most frequent collaborator.

It's probably the track that best exemplifies *Excitable Boy*, as it captures the heartfelt sentiment of 'Accidently Like A Martyr' and 'Tenderness On The Block', while simultaneously suggesting the bloodshed that permeates the 'terror trilogy'. While no one is explicitly knee-deep in gore, lines like 'I heard Woodrow Wilson's guns' and 'If you stay, you'll all be slain' hint at the historical violence that left between 200 to 1,200 Mexicans dead, compared to only 20 Americans.

Musically, Zevon aims for cultural authenticity to match lyrical accuracy, from the solemn opening recorders through Calderón's Spanish lyrics to, most especially, the use of indigenous instruments the jarano and the jaracho in the song's conclusion. The sombre subject matter is further served by one of Zevon's absolute best vocal performances, the velvet growl plunging impossibly deep on every other line.

'Veracruz' is one of Zevon's most beautiful songs, and it should automatically warrant inclusion on any 'best of' compilation; it is astonishing that this has never been the case. It's tempting to say it's also one of the great geopolitical songs of the late 1970s, but the truth is, no one else was writing material like this then.

'Tenderness On The Block' (Jackson Browne, Zevon)

According to guitarist and album co-producer Waddy Wachtel, neither 'Tenderness On The Block' nor 'Lawyers, Guns and Money' were yet part of the album, their places occupied by a reworked 'Tule's Blues' and new song 'Frozen Notes'. But Wachtel deemed those two songs to be out of kilter with the new record's more volatile tone, just as Jackson Browne had felt songs like 'Excitable Boy' and 'Werewolves Of London' upset the first album's literary apple cart. So Wachtel gave Zevon a couple of weeks to come up with replacements.

The songwriting credit further demonstrates Zevon's generosity when giving kudos to others; by Browne's own admission, he 'might have written the first two lines' before passing out from trying to keep pace with Warren's alcohol consumption. 'When I woke up, it was a song'.

Built around Zevon's piano arpeggio, and featuring the Gentlemen Boys' lush harmonies, the song is like an old friend giving good advice on the importance of parents' recognising their daughters' rights to, and rites of, independence while growing up. It's safe to assume the 1976 birth of Zevon's daughter Ariel might've been an influencing factor in the song's genesis.

'Lawyers, Guns And Money' (Zevon)

Dark, humorous and with just a soupçon of impending mayhem, this is classic Zevon, featuring a protagonist prone to a spot of bother, forever beseeching his father to send the titular resources to bail him out. The song starts with a killer Cold War couplet, 'Well, I went home with a waitress/The way I always do/How was I to know/She was with the Russians too?', before Zevon throws in another couple of then-political hotspots – Havana and Honduras – to add to those in 'Roland The Headless Thompson Gunner'.

A short sharp rocker that's already fading by the time it romps over the three-minute mark, 'Lawyers, Guns and Money' allows Waddy Wachtel to flex his muscles, laying down a stuttering guitar under the verses while allowing another to scream through a solo to great effect. When the shit hits the fan in the final line, reverb-heavy handclaps usher the song to its conclusion.

Like 'Werewolves Of London', this was a fifteen-minute job written on the back of a cocktail napkin, in this case, after Zevon realised he and friend Burt Stein were being set up as accomplices to a spot of housebreaking while on holiday in Hawaii. According to Warren's sleeve notes for the *I'll Sleep When I'm Dead* anthology, he, imagining a telegram sent to label president Joe Smith, turned to Stein and said, 'Dear Joe, send lawyers'. Stein replied, "And guns", to which Zevon added 'And Money'. In real life, none were required, Zevon and Stein successfully extricating themselves from the Laurel and Hardy-esque mess they'd gotten themselves into.

The song became a concert staple for the rest of Zevon's career, and posthumously appeared as the theme tune for the US TV series *Justice*, which ran for thirteen episodes in 2006.

Bonus Tracks
'I Need A Truck' (Zevon)
The 2007 Rhino edition came with four bonus tracks, alternative versions of the three previously released tracks listed below, and 'I Need A Truck', the only number totally new to the Zevonista faithful. Unfortunately, there's not a lot to get excited about, as the song is only 47 seconds long and takes the form of a two-verse spiritual, sung *a cappella*.

'Werewolves Of London' (Alternate version) (Marinell, Wachtel, Zevon)
The main difference between this and the album version is that it's a rough working mix, but one that allows better appreciation of John McVie's full-blooded bass-playing (assuming it's also he and Mick Fleetwood on this version). Wachtel's guitar is more in the background, where it makes suitably scratchy sounds but fails to fill the spaces.

The other notable change is the instructions ('Bite down', 'Walk tall' and 'Come down') that Zevon barks throughout this take; the only one to survive the cut was 'Draw blood', and even then, it was relegated to the fade. Finally, the London branch of Trader Vic's is correctly located in the Hilton, and the werewolf is 'dressed to the nines', as well as having perfect hair.

'Tule's Blues' (Zevon)

Zevon was reportedly unhappy about the re-release of *Wanted Dead or Alive*, but his seeming disdain for his earlier work didn't prevent him from reworking one of that album's songs for possible inclusion on *Excitable Boy*. In this new version, Zevon throws out all the country-rock trappings and slows the pace considerably, accompanied only by piano. It's still a great track, even in this fig-leaf-sporting version, but Wachtel was right to leave it off *Excitable Boy*, as it would've brought the album to a crashing halt.

'Frozen Notes' (Zevon)

Another vocal/piano song, here enlivened by a string quartet and Don Henley's impeccable vocal harmonies. If this and 'Tule's Blues' were indeed Zevon and Jackson Browne's original choice to close *Excitable Boy*, then Waddy Wachtel totally earned his co-producer fee by replacing them with 'Tenderness On The Block' and 'Lawyers, Guns And Money.'

'Frozen Notes' has great faux-Romantic lines, such as 'Looking through my window at the dark and troubled sky/I think I see the ship of the brokenhearted passing by', but there's no escaping the fact it's a tad maudlin and too similar in tone to its projected predecessor, 'Tule's Blues'. *Excitable Boy* is too boisterous an album to end on such a depressing note, frozen or otherwise.

Bad Luck Streak in Dancing School (1980)

Personnel:
Warren Zevon: vocals, piano, string synthesizer, guitar, harmonica, organ, strings
Waddy Wachtel: guitar on 'A Certain Girl' and 'Empty-Handed Heart'
Leland Sklar: bass
Rick Marotta: drums, tubular bells
David Lindley: lap steel and guitar on 'Bad Luck Street In Dancing School', 'Play It All Night' and 'Wild Age'
Joe Walsh: lead guitar on 'Jungle Work' and 'Jeannie Needs A Shooter'
Don Felder: guitar on 'A Certain Girl'
Jorge Calderón: guitar on 'A Certain Girl'
Jackson Browne: guitars on 'Gorilla, You're A Desperado'
Ben Keith: pedal steel on 'Bed Of Coals'
Sid Sharp: concertmaster
Backing vocals: Jackson Browne, Rick Marotta, Jorge Calderón, Linda Ronstadt, Glenn Frey, J. D. Souther, Don Henley, Warren Zevon
Producers: Greg Ladanyi, Warren Zevon
Recorded at The Sound Factory, Los Angeles,
Release date: 15 February 1980
Label: Asylum
Chart placing: US: 20
Running time: 35:31

After *Excitable Boy* was released, Dave Marsh's *Rolling Stone* feature on Warren Zevon made this quietly ominous observation: 'Zevon takes another sip of his "phlegm cutter", a couple of fingers of Stolichnaya vodka with which he's been dosing himself all afternoon'. Zevon now had in his grasp the success he'd worked more than a decade for, but, ravaged by alcoholism, he was in no fit state to hold onto it. Even worse, he either started living up to the 'werewolf' and 'excitable boy' nicknames bestowed upon him by a music press yet unaware of his illness, or he really was every bit as dangerous as the characters in those two ragtime penny dreadfuls.

His behaviour alienated his colleagues, with Jackson Browne and Waddy Wachtel both deciding against producing the *Excitable Boy* follow-up (To their credit, they remained friends with Zevon and still appeared on his albums, but they could live without the drama of trying to direct him). Zevon thought of Bruce Springsteen's manager and producer Jon Landau for what would become *Bad Luck Streak in Dancing School*, but Landau was aware of the singer's volatility, not least from his brother David, who played guitar on the *Excitable Boy* tour during which Zevon regularly missed his cues, fluffed his lines, took drunken stumbles onstage, showed up late, or, on one occasion, not at all. There was also an incident backstage at a Springsteen gig – which Warren attended partly to coax Jon Landau into producing his album – where an inebriated Zevon had to be calmed down and shown to his seat by

Springsteen himself, which cost The Boss his pre-gig preparation time. Seated next to *Rolling Stone* founder Jann Wenner, Zevon's subsequent behaviour resulted in Wenner banning coverage of the singer in the magazine. It seemed Zevon burned bridges wherever he went.

Far more worrying was his fascination with guns, which he started to collect and would leave loaded around the house. Escapades included using them to exterminate cockroaches (by shooting, not cudgelling); attempting to take a gun into a Jackson Browne show while singing 'Jackson Browne, shoot him down'; taking pot shots at a Richard Pryor billboard on Sunset Boulevard; and – famously – assassinating the front cover of *Excitable Boy*.

Zevon's worst nightmare was a recurring one which he only revealed much later. In his dreams, he wandered outside in a vodka-induced stupor to shoot at passing cars, but the next morning would find him gripped with terror, counting the bullets in the chamber. Real violence did also occur, as he was prone to fits of rage, with his wife Crystal the target of his verbal and physical abuse. They separated before the 1970s were done, but not before she had convinced him to seek professional help for his disease.

It took another five or so years, but eventually, Zevon and his new best pal sobriety became inseparable. In the meantime, he went through the cycle of struggle and failure. He told *Rolling Stone* journalist Paul Nelson that he would storm around the house, sober but oh-so-close to abandoning the wagon, railing against himself: '"You're not a fucking *boy* and you're not a fucking *werewolf*, you're a fucking *man*, and it's about time you acted like it"'. It's safe to say Zevon was not at his most mentally robust, a situation undoubtedly exacerbated by Asylum looking for a successor to his hit album.

Bad Luck Streak in Dancing School was released in February 1980, and though some sung its praises – *Sounds*' Sandy Robertson, for example, opining that 'It might be his best work yet' – the overall reception was one of muted positivity, the consensus being that, artistically and conceptually, it fell somewhere between *Warren Zevon* and *Excitable Boy* without quite matching either. The classical fragments robbed the album of its momentum, the new technology detracted rather than added to the sound, and, with a second song about mercenaries and a comedic number featuring another 'hairy-handed gent', there were accusations of repetition. These comments were unfair. The classical interludes not only serve as perfect introductions to the three songs they precede, but they also give the album texture and colour. Neil Young once said that despite technological advancement the music of the 1970s would age better than that of the 1980s, but Warren's use of synthesizers is understated enough to not instantly carbon-date these songs to the short-sleeved jacket decade, while their presence demonstrates on his part an awareness of then-current music trends, such as the prevalence of new wave pop bands like Blondie and The Cars, and a willingness to move more with the times than many of his Asylum labelmates. And while 'Jungle Work' and 'Gorilla, You're A Desperado' undisputedly conjured up 'Roland' and 'Werewolves' respectively, it's not as if the late-1970s/early-1980s are remembered for their glut of songs about hired guns and bewhiskered beasts. Zevon was alone in letting loose the shaggy dogs of war stories, and he didn't do it again.

Sandy Robertson's assessment above might be overstating it, but *Bad Luck Streak* is a worthy successor to the critically acclaimed darlings that came before it, and is perhaps now ripe for reappraisal. Like its predecessors, it has a mix of heartbreak and humour, of tenderness and mayhem, of rockers and ballads. As with *Warren Zevon*, *Bad Luck Streak* is the work of a songwriter willing to be both brutal and brutally honest, as evinced by 'Empty-Handed Heart' and 'Bed of Coals'. Like *Excitable Boy*, it benefits from crisp production and expert sequencing. It contains instant classics (the two aforementioned songs, 'Play It All Night Long', 'Bill Lee' and a couple of others), and two tunes best described as 'not classics' (the title track and 'Gorilla, You're A Desperado': Zevon was obviously fond of them though, as both made it onto the 1996 *I'll Sleep When I'm Dead* anthology).

Bad Luck Streak is, in other words, a Warren Zevon album, unfortunately, the last to trouble the *Billboard* top 20 for nearly a quarter of a century.

'Bad Luck Streak In Dancing School' (Zevon)

'It came to me as a kind of joke.' Zevon told Michael Branton of *Bay Area Magazine*. 'I pictured a cartoon of a guy with his arms and legs in a cast, holding a crutch, a bandage 'round his head, with the line 'Bad luck streak in dancing school''. Maybe you had to be there, because although the title track of Zevon's third Asylum album is too inoffensive to ever be anyone's least favourite song, it's also undeniably no great shakes.

After sitting out *Excitable Boy*, the Sid Sharp Strings make a welcome return, opening the track with a classical flourish (a snippet of Zevon's eternally unfinished symphony), punctuated after eighteen seconds by the unmistakable sound of gunfire, two shots courtesy of Warren's .44 Magnum, a swaggering self-indulgence from a group of seasoned musicians apparently unfamiliar with the humble handclap. The gun is replaced by an axe, also wielded by Warren, who fills the post-shots silence with tough, surly guitar. He's soon joined by Leland Sklar and Rick Marotta, who, unusually, stick around for the entire album, making this the first Zevon long player to have a fixed rhythm section. Marotta's drums are the track highlight, keeping time by being wonderfully all-over-the-place in the verses, settling into a more traditional role when the chorus arrives. Meanwhile, David Lindley's lap steel skitters around the fringes, always making its presence felt but never aiming for centre stage.

The lyric is pure autobiography. It might be dressed up as sex addiction with a bit of BDSM thrown in for good measure – 'Dancing School' being a euphemism for a bordello – but it's about alcoholism. The singer has been 'breaking all the rules' and 'acting like a fool', but now he's 'Down on my knees in pain'. But like many a man who has erred, he swears to God he'll change, pleading 'Pauline, don't make me beg'. Replace Pauline with Crystal, and the lyrics present an accurate description of where Zevon was at the time of writing. Alcoholism and squandered love are themes that deserve a stronger tune than the lumbering brute they are shackled to here. Fortunately, later in the album, that's exactly what they get.

'A Certain Girl' (Naomi Neville aka Allen Toussaint)

This first appeared as the B-side of Ernie K-Doe's minor 1961 US hit 'I Cried A Tear', and three years later was the flipside of The Yardbirds' debut single 'I Wish You Would'. It finally achieved A-side status when released as this album's lead single, but only reached a disappointing 57, and was Zevon's last US hit single.

Zevon discards the original's piano-driven formula in favour of a triple-guitar approach, The Eagles' Don Felder joining regular cohorts Wachtel and Calderón. This new arrangement transcends the original's blues roots, and transforms the song into a rockier barroom boogie, albeit one with a highly-polished pop production. It fits the album well, the only missing component being the hootin' and a-hollerin' that surely accompanied the studio session.

'Jungle Work' (Jorge Calderón, Zevon)

The mood gets heavier with Zevon's second hymn glorifying the mercenary, in which Roland's surviving comrades soldier on.

The grinding guitar and pulsing bass ominously suggest the lyric's approaching menace: 'Lear jet SWAT team/On the midnight run/With the M16/ And the Ingram gun'. The lyric is the movie *The Wild Geese* condensed into a four-minute pop song, with Zevon (or Calderón) offering up his most obscure geopolitical location to date with Ovamboland. The narrative is all very tight and thrilling, the only stumble being the frankly gravity-defying second act in the couplet 'We parachute in/We parachute out'. After paying vocal tribute to 'strength and muscle and jungle work', Zevon, Calderón and Marotta join in humming something that really does sound quite hymnal, their harmonies perhaps reflecting camaraderie under fire.

Joe Walsh provides a screaming lead guitar approximating the 'death from above' promised in the words, while nothing screams '1980s' quite as much as the deployment of such wonderfully-dated former instruments of tomorrow as the string synthesizer and the Syndrum. Fortunately, both are used with restraint, but be warned that Marotta's electronic drum sound is not easily dislodged once it burrows into the ear canal.

'Empty-Handed Heart' (Zevon)

Zevon again demonstrates his skill in crafting exquisite love songs. This is the squandered love song alluded to earlier, written for Crystal after their separation. Zevon is left wondering if he'll make it without the woman who's been his wife, friend, lover, forgiver and, at times, carer, and determines that he will, even acknowledging that he's met someone else he cares for. Thus emboldened, he encourages Crystal to rebuild her life ('Leave the fire behind you and start'), but the truth lies embedded in a line placed at the song's centre: 'No one will ever take the place of you'.

Zevon told Jim Sullivan of the *Boston Globe* that he cleared the studio when recording this vocal, saying he 'needed to re-experience the emotional context of the song'. His delivery is as faultless as it is heart-wrenching, his voice full of loss and regret, almost breaking as he delivers the line 'If after all is said and done/You only find one special one', before Linda Ronstadt's warm vocal adds a ghostly reminder of how good life together once was.

Except for a brief and clever burst of bass and drums, verse one consists solely of piano. When the other musicians join in, they do so with restraint, leaving the spotlight on Zevon. The songwriter doesn't disappoint, his playing matching the lyric's beauty while eschewing the traditional verse-chorus-verse for something more structurally unusual.

Three years after Zevon's passing, his last record label Artemis released a collection variously called *Romantic Genius* or *The Love Songs*, depending on the country of release. Not surprisingly, the focus was on tracks Warren recorded while with Artemis, but some earlier songs were included. The fact that 'Empty-Handed Heart' is not among them is astonishing, as it's one of his very best heartbreakers.

'Interlude No. 1' (Zevon)

Though identified as a separate track on the album sleeve, 'Interlude No. 1', another snapshot of Zevon's symphony-in-progress, is gone in 26 seconds, and serves as an introduction to the next track.

'Play It All Night Long' (Zevon)

This completes the informal trilogy begun with 'Mohammed's Radio' and 'Johnny Strikes Up the Band' about the redemptive power of music, but it is considerably bleaker and more desperate than its forebears. A withering, almost gothic ode to rural living, the song bypasses the bucolic idyll presented by many a Southern and West Coast rocker, going straight for the grimmer realities of incest, madness, senility, alcoholism and illness (both human and bovine). The only escape is to 'Turn those speakers up full blast' and 'Play that dead band's song', the song being 'Sweet Home Alabama' by Lynyrd Skynyrd, three members of whom died in a plane crash in October 1977.

Many reviewers have suggested that 'Play It All Night Long' is laced with Zevon's brand of black-hearted humour, but the singer was having none of it, as he told the *Boston Globe*: 'It's not intended as a ridicule of Lynyrd Skynyrd. I don't think it's funny that rock stars get killed in plane crashes'.

Despite its harrowing southern gothic subject matter, which shares its DNA with the works of Flannery O'Connor and Harry Crews, 'Play It All Night Long' is surprisingly rousing. The song is anchored with a string-synthesizer ostinato which has weathered the test of time well, and it benefits from Rick Marotta's splendid drumming. But the star of the show is David Lindley, an in-demand studio and touring player and a recording artist in his own right. He appeared on *Warren Zevon* and was to guest on many subsequent Zevon albums, but his exhilarating, incandescent soloing on this track might just be his finest contribution to the Zevon canon. The only downside is the indecent haste with which the track proceeds to its fade-out, cutting off Lindley's string wizardry while he's still casting his spell.

This track cropped up on all three 'best of' compilations released in Zevon's lifetime, and rightly so; it's an absolute gem.

'Jeannie Needs A Shooter' (Bruce Springsteen, Zevon)

Through mutual friend Jon Landau, Zevon had heard Bruce Springsteen was working on a song called 'Janey Needs A Shooter'. Zevon loved the title, asking how the song was coming along each time he saw Springsteen. Eventually the Boss, who had never gone beyond naming the song, bequeathed the title to Zevon, telling him that if he liked it so much, he should write it. Which he did. This is the more prevalent version of the story. Another, told in C. M. Kushins' *Nothing's Bad Luck: The Lives of Warren Zevon*, is that Zevon wrote some of it, played it to Springsteen, and they finished the song together. In yet another, T Bone Burnett also tinkered with it. The most often-told first option seems the most plausible. Zevon had previously credited Jackson Browne on 'Tenderness On The Block', when Browne, by his own admission, had only contributed the first couple of lines. David Lindell got a co-write on 'Nighttime In The Switching Yard' because he had chatted about trains with Zevon some years earlier in Spain. So it would be in Zevon's character to acknowledge Springsteen as co-creator of 'Jeannie Needs A Shooter' if he supplied the title and the inspiration, and, applying the same standard, unlikely for Zevon to not give Burnett credit if he contributed some lyrics.

The lyric suggests we are back in the Old West of 'A Bullet For Ramona' and 'Frank And Jessie James', and tells of the protagonist's attempt to elope with the sheriff's daughter. Lines like 'She came down from Knightstown with her hands hard from the line' and 'We met down by the river on the final day of May' certainly smack of Springsteen, but it's more likely to be Warren 'doing a Bruce', much as he would later on 'Roll With The Punches'. On the other hand, the violence that concludes 'Jeannie Needs A Shooter' – the narrator shot in the back and left to die in the rainswept night – is Zevon at his most pulpy.

The Sid Sharp Strings are back to lend this mid-tempo rocker an anthemic quality, and Joe Walsh also lays down more sterling lead guitar. Kudos must also go to Rick Marotta, whose use of tubular bells gives the track a distinctive identity.

Springsteen finished his own version of the song decades later when 'Janey Needs A Shooter' cropped up on his 2020 album *Letter to You*.

'Interlude No. 2' (Zevon)
This is the final tantalising snatch of Zevon's incomplete symphony. It's quite lovely and, like the previous excerpt, segues nicely into the next song.

'Bill Lee' (Zevon)
Written from the point of view of outspoken Boston Red Sox/Montreal Expos pitcher Bill 'Spaceman' Lee, this is a non-romantic ballad with attitude. It's essentially a solo number, Zevon providing voice, piano, and a harmonica with a bad case of the blues, his only support coming from Glenn Frey on vocal harmonies. At only 1:35 in length it's the album's shortest song, but what it lacks in length, it more than makes up for in charisma. It also marks Warren's entry into a new genre, the sports song, to which he was to return on future albums.

Zevon wasn't the only rock act to immortalise Bill Lee, as he was also the subject of 'What Bothers The Spaceman' by Mono Puff, a side project of They Might Be Giants frontman John Flansburgh.

'Gorilla, You're A Desperado' (Zevon)
This is Zevon's second simian song, after 'Gorilla' from his 1969 debut, and with its hirsute title character and tongue-in-cheek lyric, it could also be seen as a successor to 'Werewolves Of London'. Asylum certainly thought so, and released it as the album's third and final single. Had it been a hit, it would surely have left Zevon irredeemably tarred as a novelty artist. Perhaps with hindsight, the glint of silver linings shines brighter than the gleam of silver dollars.

This is not to say it's a bad song. The words, a satire of how tough it is for well-to-do Angelenos with too much time to think about themselves, are fun, if occasionally overwrought. But musically, this is a slice of bright, sparkly sunshine pop, guaranteed to put a spring in the step. It comes stacked with considerable star power too, with Jackson Browne ably demonstrating that David Lindley isn't the only double-denim dude handy with a slide guitar, and Browne, J. D. Souther and Don Henley supplying effortlessly brilliant harmonies.

'Bed Of Coals' (T Bone Burnett, Zevon)
If 'Carmelita' was a junkie's lament, 'Bed Of Coals' is the coronach of the alcoholic, its stark lyrics lived rather than imagined. This could only be written by someone with the newfound clarity that alcoholism is a disease, and that it's killing him.

A slow country waltz with honky-tonk piano, Zevon corrals yet another outstanding pedal steel maestro in Ben Keith, who by this stage had played on half a dozen Neil Young records and would appear on many more. Keith's contribution is essential, his playing providing heartache with heart, and Sklar and Marotta are typically stellar.

But the voices are what really lift the song, giving it a hymnal quality, with J. D. Souther sharing harmonies with a returning Linda Ronstadt, whose heartfelt delivery all but drowns Souther out. Outshining them both is Zevon himself, the vinyl grooves reeking of Stolichnaya, stale Marlboros and utter despair, as he realises he's 'too old to die young/And too young to die now'. His emotive vocal puts the ache in heartache.

'Bed Of Coals' is Zevon's most acute heartbreaker, a thing of beauty and wild desperation. You *will* feel every needle that pierced through his heart.

'Wild Age' (Zevon)

This opens with a Romantic evocation of youth:

You've seen him leaning on the streetlight
Listening to some song inside
You've seen him standing by the highway
Trying to hitch a ride'

It then revels in its seeming invincibility: 'And the law can't stop 'em/No one can stop 'em/At the wild age', before conceding that a life of recklessness comes with a price, as 'Some of them keep running/'Til they run straight in their graves'. Artfully written, with a clear narrative focus, it's almost a form of poetic journalism, but it also seems rather odd that the newly / nearly sober Zevon is already mythologising his recently-recanted press personas, the Excitable Boy and the Werewolf of Los Angeles. Nonetheless, it's another top song, a perfect album closer and possibly an excellent showstopper.

David Lindley is back on guitar, offering a performance that nearly rivals his work on 'Play It All Night Long', his mournful playing balancing the eulogia of the lyrics. Leland Sklar, whose playing has been too muted in many of the preceding tracks, is given space to flex here, and provides a solid and unfussy rock around which Lindley's guitar bends and whistles like the wind. As ever, some of Southern California's finest are on hand to supply typically exquisite harmonies – in this instance, Glenn Frey and Don Henley – freeing Zevon up to holler through the close, playing for fun the role he admitted in 'Bed Of Coals' that he could no longer play for real.

The Envoy (1982)

Personnel:
Warren Zevon: vocals, piano, guitar, synthesizer, electric piano
Waddy Wachtel: guitars, percussion
David Landau: guitars
Danny Kortchmar: guitar on 'Ain't That Pretty At All'
LeRoy P. Marinell: acoustic guitar on 'Ain't That Pretty At All'
Kenny Edwards: guitar on 'Looking For The Next Best Thing'
Leland Sklar, Bob Glaub: bass
Jeff Porcaro: drums, Tahitian log drums, pule sticks
Mike Botts: drums on 'Ain't That Pretty At All'
Steve Forman: percussion on 'Ain't That Pretty At All'
Rick Marotta: drums on 'Charlie's Medicine'
Russell Kunkel: drums on 'Never Too Late For Love'
Harmony vocals: Don Henley, Lindsey Buckingham, Jordan Zevon, Jorge Calderón,
Waddy Wachtel, David Landau, J. D. Souther, Graham Nash, Warren Zevon
Producers: Warren Zevon, Greg Ladanyi, Waddy Wachtel
Recorded at Record One, Los Angeles
Release date: 16 July 1982
Label: Asylum
Chart placing: US: 93
Running time: 31:59

The 1980s started well for Warren. *Bad Luck Streak* was released in February, and, while not the big seller *Excitable Boy* had been, it was doing well. Also doing well, for now at least, was his battle with the bottle. He and sobriety weren't yet in a monogamous relationship – that milestone lay a few years down the line – but battle had at least commenced, and Zevon was scoring a few wins. To enable continuing success, he had thrown himself into a fitness regime that incorporated karate and dance lessons (the latter inspiring the joke whose punchline, in turn, inspired *Bad Luck Streak*'s title). Less positively, he had also turned to what he regarded as 'controlled' substance abuse to negate his need for alcohol, with painkillers and cocaine becoming two of his new best buds, with the occasional heroin dalliance thrown in for not-so-good measure.

His relationship with actress Kim Lankford, then at the height of her fame playing Ginger Ward on *Dallas* spin-off *Knots Landing*, found him unexpectedly becoming one half of a Hollywood golden couple, which, among other perks, allowed him to socialise with the likes of Clint Eastwood and Martin Scorsese. Being a fan of both, this presented no hardship, except perhaps the ongoing requirement to keep one's inner fanboy well and truly buttoned. Meanwhile, over on the East Coast, Warren struck up an important and lasting friendship with David Letterman.

The Zevon that toured the States to support *Bad Luck Streak* was significantly different from the one that had toured *Excitable Boy*. Gone was the often-incoherent guy with a penchant for falling off the piano stool, the stage, or falling down drunk. In his place was a lean, fit and fully-focussed performer presenting a (eventually) bare-chested, sweat-drenched and adrenaline-fuelled show that had the audience up out of their seats and dancing. There were some sniffy reviews from critics that didn't think this was how an Asylum artist should act, but the tour was critically lauded overall, and the five-show finale at The Roxy in L.A. was recorded for posterity. The resultant album *Stand in the Fire* was released in the last week of 1980 to overwhelmingly positive reviews.

Despite all this, Asylum were watching their pennies, particularly with artists who weren't selling according to expectation. Instead of financing a tour of Europe, where Zevon had an established following, the record company instead sent him over to play what friend and road manager George Gruel called 'every European version of *American Bandstand'*. Worse, there would be no band, and even Zevon himself wasn't permitted to play live but instead had to mime to pre-recorded versions of the same three songs per show. Asylum's lack of support in promoting both *Bad Luck Streak* and *Stand in the Fire,* must have rankled, but the European jaunt had a side effect as rewarding as it was unexpected. Zevon, for whom songwriting was a form of torture, suddenly found himself on an uncharacteristic creative streak, and the next album quickly began to take shape.

The Envoy is the often overlooked Zevon album, and unfairly so, as, barring one notable exception, this is a fine collection of songs. It's true there's nothing quite as outstanding as 'Roland The Headless Thompson Gunner' or 'Desperados Under the Eaves' here, but that's not to say there's nothing of note. From the stadium-rock-ready title track, through the hymnal 'Jesus Mentioned', the starkly beautiful 'Never Too Late For Love', the out-of-its-skull 'Ain't That Pretty At All', to the luminous 'The Hula Hula Boys', there is plenty of shade and texture on offer, and much to admire.

Reviews were mixed. Writing in *Sounds*, the ever-dependable Sandy Robertson rather alarmingly began his review with 'Asylum Records really should just get rid of Warren Zevon', before laying down the punchline, 'He's so good, he shows up just how dire everyone else on the label really is'. John Metzgar writing in *The Music Box* upon the 2007 release of the CD, stated that *The Envoy* "boasted a stylistic breadth that was unlike anything (Zevon) had ever concocted". Mark Deming, writing retroactively on AllMusic, was more representative of the critical consensus: 'When Zevon confronts his own demons on *The Envoy*, the album is intense and compelling stuff, but unfortunately, there aren't enough of these moments to prop up the rest of the set, which is smart and literate, but not especially exciting'.

The Envoy only reached 93 in the US, a vertiginous plummet compared to the number 20 spot secured by *Bad Luck Streak*. Though said in jest, Sandy Robertson got his wish, and Asylum dropped Zevon, the singer only discovering this in the cruellest way possible, by reading about it in *Rolling Stone*.

'The Envoy' (Zevon)

Those hoping for a third song about soldiers of fortune would've been disappointed when the title track clearly signalled that the mercenaries were out, and the mediator was in. The envoy in question is Philip Habib (1920 - 1992), whose superior negotiating skills saved the life of future South Korean president Kim Dae-jung in 1973, averted a war between Israel and Syria in 1981, and ended the siege of Beirut in 1982. Warren had perhaps wised up to the fact that the pen is indeed mightier than the sword.

That said, 'The Envoy' displays as much if not more musical firepower than 'Jungle Work'. Occupying the drum stool for most of the album is Toto's Jeff Porcaro, then at the height of his powers, enjoying the phenomenal success of the multi-platinum *Toto IV*. He kick-starts the opening number with an artful clatter, and then keeps time by bludgeoning it gracefully. Waddy Wachtel, David Landau and Zevon all play guitar, with Zevon unusually being allowed to do the soloing. Years earlier, LeRoy Marinell had explained to Zevon that no one let him play his own guitar solos because he was far too excitable. 'Well, I'm just an excitable boy', replied Zevon, and a song was born. Perhaps now getting to play his own solos is why he told *Rolling Stone*'s Mikal Gilmore that he viewed his new platter as '*Excitable Boy* grows up'. Zevon also remains enamoured with the synthesizer, but again, his use of it remains tasteful; it, along with Leland Sklar's redoubtable bass, adds to the song's stridency without embarrassingly dating it. Finally, this track is Zevon's only outing on a prepared piano, which, for those unfamiliar with the term, involves temporarily altering the sound of the piano by placing cutlery, bolts, screws, and other objects between the strings.

Lyrically, we're embedded in the geopolitical landscape of the early 1980s, with things getting 'hot in El Salvador', 'guns in Damascus' and 'Nuclear arms in the Middle East'. In other words, we're in the world of Philip Habib, who sent Zevon a thank-you note written on State Department stationary, for his efforts.

'The Overdraft' (Thomas McGuane, Zevon)

Like the title track, 'The Overdraft' is another big-sound rocker, a perfect set opener, and purpose-built for all those stadiums Warren would never play. It starts in a hurry and never lets up, leaving the listener playing catch-up for the duration of its fiery, sub-three-minute running time. Zevon's back on the piano, mercilessly tickling the upper ivories, a nice contrast to Wachtel and Laundau's crunchy guitar chords. Waddy also plays a ferocious solo in the middle, with a reprise at the coda. The song's maniacal pace is best exemplified by Lindsey Buckingham's spectacularly bonkers harmony vocals, the increasingly idiosyncratic Fleetwood Mac man sounding as if he showed up at the studio after a particularly high intake of sugar. Fortunately, Sklar and Porcaro are there to temper the song's gleeful exuberance without suppressing it completely.

Co-written with novelist Thomas McGuane, the lyric is oblique, short on verse, and too quick to get to the chorus. Despite its parentage, it can hardly be described as literary, and there is absolutely nothing to distinguish McGuane's contribution.

'The Hula Hula Boys' (Zevon)

This is a humorous sex romp about a hapless cuckold on honeymoon in Hawaii with a new wife that would rather spend her time with the hotel's car park attendant or 'The fat one from the swimming pool'. Even the chorus is a joke – the lyrics 'Ha'ina i' a mai ana ka puana' being a Hawaiian idiom meaning 'Get to the essential point' (or perhaps in the case of a song, 'Sing the chorus').

The slight, lighthearted lyrical tone perfectly suits the musical accompaniment while being simultaneously at odds with it. The compatibility stems from a lilting melody immediately suggestive of the story's location, with Jeff Porcaro's Tahitian log drums and pule sticks and Jim Horn's recorders providing a cultural flavour. Zevon's dreamy descending piano chords are the musical equivalent of a majestic sun slowly sinking into the reddening Pacific. The discordance between words and music occurs because the shimmering, gorgeous sunshine pop arrangement is far too beautiful for the frothy, borderline-crass lyrics it supports. That it works at all is down to Zevon's straight-faced and, at times, lachrymose vocal delivery; lyrics such as 'I didn't have to come to Maui/To be treated like a jerk' may be jokey, but the protagonist's emotions are not.

'Jesus Mentioned' (Zevon)

Zevon often referred to himself as a folk singer, and 'Jesus Mentioned' is an out-and-out folk song, albeit one unlikely to ever be covered by Peter, Paul and Mary. Accompanied only by Waddy Wachtel providing warm, woody fretwork, this is a spiritual that conflates Jesus with Elvis and confuses resurrectionism with the Resurrection.

The song starts off reverently enough, with the narrator heading to Graceland in Memphis, Tennessee, 'Thinking about the King/Remembering him sing/About those heavenly mansions Jesus mentioned'. Things take a turn for the sinister when the gravedigging inclinations last seen on 'Excitable Boy' are revealed, the protagonist now stating his intentions of 'Digging up the King/Begging him to sing'.

'Jesus Mentioned' could be Zevon's legendary black humour at play, but it could equally be seen as an observation on the price of fame and the obsession of fans. Exhuming your idol might seem a stretch, but prior to 8 December 1980, so too did shooting them four times in the back, and this song was composed in the wake of John Lennon's murder.

'Let Nothing Come Between You' (Zevon)

This was *The Envoy*'s only single, and though it reached 24 on *Billboard*'s Mainstream Rock chart (a chart measuring success on rock radio stations), it didn't trouble any sales-based chart.

It's an autobiographical number about Zevon's relationship with Kim Lankford. The couple told *People* magazine of their intention to wed, so in the lyric, Zevon duly notes that he's 'Got the license, got the ring/Got back the blood tests and everything'. Earlier, he tells us he 'went to see my friend to ask his advice/He just smiled and said, 'She's good around the eyes'', this being precisely what Jackson Browne had said after being introduced to Lankford. So, the man was in love, and who would deny him that or the optimism expressed in this song, but the whole thing is hampered by a banal nonsense de-di-de vocal hook that repeats way more than should be allowed in any one song.

Leland Sklar's silky bass sets the ball rolling, Toto's Steve Lukather fills in for a missing David Landau, and the whole piece is impeccably produced, but there is no escaping that 'Let Nothing Come Between You' is a plodding slice of Yacht Rock with the twee dial ramped up way too high.

'Ain't That Pretty At All' (LeRoy P. Marinell, Zevon)

The original vinyl's side-two opener is a kaleidoscope of rock's different decades compressed into one song. The twanging guitar that serves in lieu of a chorus is lifted straight from Duane Eddy (circa 1958); the bratty vocals, spat rather than sung, reminiscent of first-wave London punks such as the Sex Pistols and X-Ray Spex; and the demented fairground synthesizer sound that plays throughout could only hail from the 1980s.

The gonzo lyrics are eminently quotable, from the 'I'm going to hurl myself against the wall/Because I'd rather feel bad than not feel anything at all' to the 'Oh, how'd you like it?', and though they are credited with backing vocals, J. D. Souther and Waddy Wachtel merely join in at the end in a bid to outshout Zevon, before the vocals give way once more to the spectral presence of the King of Twang.

'It Ain't That Pretty At All' might seem to be a bit of a throwaway, but it's a fun rocker that counters the saccharine that slathered the previous track, and perhaps offers insight into Zevon's perilous state of mind as he fought to stave off the old addiction while grappling with the new.

'Charlie's Medicine' (Zevon)

Charlie was a real person, and he used to sell Zevon pharmaceuticals, legitimate prescriptions, according to biographer C. M. Kushins, though this suggestion of respectability is punctured in the very next sentence, which quotes George Gruel saying he and Warren used to go to Charlie's house to acquire 'bags of these pink downers'. Charlie was murdered outside his Fairfax Avenue home, though Gruel doesn't confirm whether the shooter was indeed 'some respectable doctor from Beverly Hills'.

Appropriately for a song based on such a violent crime, 'Charlie's Medicine' starts with a menace-suffused acoustic leitmotif, a ready-made soundtrack for some noir detective show. The spidery guitar is soon joined by easy, jazzy, Sunday afternoon-slot drums and bass, supplied by the old team of Bob Glaub and Rick Marotta, before rocking out at the beginning of the second verse. Waddy Wachtel earns his 'Axe Hero' t-shirt with a feisty solo, before the song returns to the first verse and its attendant Bourbon Street shuffle.

Despite knowing the victim, Zevon sings with a detachment that's entirely in keeping with the piece's noir spirit. The phrases 'poor kid' and 'I'm sorry Charlie died' are expressed without emotion, although Zevon did attend the real Charlie's funeral.

'Looking For The Next Best Thing' (Kenny Edwards, Marinell, Zevon)

Jeff Porcaro is back behind the kit, and he really likes to be heard first, whether via the preemptive drum fill that kicks off the title track or the whispering cymbal that introduces 'The Hula Hula Boys'. Here he is again, the listener's first contact with 'Looking For The Next Best Thing', an initially undemanding but pleasing-enough song about appreciating the best but settling for less.

But it isn't Mister Porcaro that sells the song, and it certainly isn't Warren's most Eighties synth sound to date, one not too far removed tonally from that later heard on Van Halen's 'Jump'. Wachtel lets rip another solo scorcher, and J. D Souther and Graham Nash's harmonies are every bit as impeccable as you would expect, but neither of these are the clincher either. The thing that elevates this track from being merely a pleasant placeholder is the devastatingly sublime pause that falls around the 1:57 mark, just after the truly lovely ascending synthisizer chords that follow Waddy's solo. The line immediately after this says, 'All alone on the road to perfection', but, really, with that small pop masterstroke, Zevon shows he had already arrived.

'Never Too Late For Love' (Zevon)

The previous two albums ended with bad-ass rockers in the shape of 'Lawyers, Guns, and Money' and 'Wild Age', so Zevon here switches gears and delivers another of his superior ballads. The song is musically elegiac but lyrically brimming with optimism, and whereas phrases such as 'Don't stop believing in tomorrow' might come across as air-punching sloganeering in lesser hands, Zevon delivers with absolute sincerity.

The song builds up layer by layer, very softly to begin with, just piano, then voice (Zevon's vocal here is particularly strong), gradually joined by acoustic guitar, bass, drums and electric guitars, which by the time the solo arrives, have graduated to producing Townshend-style down-stroked power chords. Having started the album with three guitarists on the opening track, we're now down to Wachtel playing (at least) three guitars, the acoustic that adds autumnal warmth throughout, and a couple of electrics.

This song really should've cropped up on future compilation albums, but the fact it didn't makes it a bit of an overlooked gem, an appellation that could equally be applied to several of the tracks on this fine album.

Bonus Tracks
'Word Of Mouth' (Zevon)

Sometimes bonus tracks add value and sometimes they do not, and this is a prime example of the latter. It's a song that never made it to the lyric stage and is suspiciously lacking in melody too. As such, it could probably have served as the theme to an Aaron Spelling production from the 1970s, but everyone else will give it one listen and forever press 'skip' thereafter.

'Let Nothing Come Between You' (Alternate version) (Zevon)

Warren tries out some funny voices throughout, and a spot of yodelling creeps in at the end, so yes, this is an infinitely worse version of the song you already hated.

'The Risk'

This, on the other hand, is one of those bonus tracks that *does* add value. It hasn't progressed beyond the demo stage, would benefit from a middle eight and concluding verse, and the synthesisers and drums make it as much a child of the Eighties as a slap bracelet, but there is a good tune here, one ripe for cultivation. With a bit more TLC, this would not have been far removed from such synth-driven pop classics as 'Girls Just Want To Have Fun' or 'Dancing In The Dark', and might even have enjoyed some MTV rotation. 'Should have done, should have done, we all sigh'.

'Wild Thing' (Chip Taylor)

This version of the Troggs classic was presumably just a bit of studio tomfoolery that was never meant to see the light of day, yet here we are.

Sentimental Hygiene (1987)

Personnel:
Warren Zevon: vocals, piano, keyboards, guitar, Emulator
Peter Buck: guitar
Mike Mills: bass
Bill Berry: drums-
Neil Young: lead guitar on 'Sentimental Hygiene'
Waddy Wachtel: guitar on 'Sentimental Hygiene', 'Reconsider Me', 'Even A Dog Can Shake Hands' and 'The Heartache'
Jorge Calderón: bass on 'Sentimental Hygiene'
Bob Dylan: harmonica on 'The Factory'
Brian Setzer: lead guitar on 'Trouble Waiting To Happen'
Mike Campbell: guitar on 'Reconsider Me'
Jai Winding: keyboard on 'Reconsider Me'
Tony Levin: bass on 'Reconsider Me'
Craig Krampf: drums on 'Reconsider Me' and 'Leave My Monkey Alone'
David Lindley: lap steel on 'Detox Mansion'; bowed saz on 'Bad Karma'
Darius Degher: sitar on 'Bad Karma'
Rick Richards: guitar on 'Even A Dog Can Shake Hands'
Leland Sklar: bass on 'The Heartache'
Blackbyrd McKnight: guitar on 'Leave My Monkey Alone'
Amp Fiddler: keyboard on 'Leave My Monkey Alone'
Flea: bass on 'Leave My Monkey Alone'
Will Alexander, Brian Bell: computer programming on 'Leave My Monkey Alone'
George Clinton: arrangement on 'Leave My Monkey Alone'
Harmony vocals: Don Henley, Jorge Calderón, Michael Stipe, Jennifer Warnes, Warren Zevon
Producers: Warren Zevon, Niko Bolas, and Andrew Slater
Recorded at Record One and A&M Studios, Los Angeles; Cheshire Sound Studios, Atlanta, Georgia
Release date: 29 August 1987
Label: Virgin
Chart Placing: US: 63
Running time: 36:49

The Zevon that had started the new decade so optimistically was starting to unravel. His romance with Kim Lankford was over, the actress recognising that some of Zevon's character traits did not a soulmate make. Blasting the apartment with his .44 Magnum was at odds with his self-proclaimed desire for a quiet, normal life, and your hubby-to-be shooting heroin with a bunch of strangers (including a certain Charlie, not long for this mortal coil) is not what you want to come home to. Finally, there was the temper and the violence. When Zevon discovered that Lankford had been invited to sing with Ray Charles at a fundraiser, he went into a rage, screaming and pulling her hair. *He* was the rock star, *he* should be singing with Ray, not her, some actress from the soaps. Meanwhile, his last record had tanked at the tills, Asylum had terminated his contract, and his sobriety – always a self-deception, Warren having substituted substance abuse for the bottle – was cast aside. Zevon faced his problems by popping the cap off the vodka, and diving in deep.

Salvation was at hand, first in the form of Andrew Slater, who, having championed Zevon when he was on the cusp of being dropped by his artist representation company, suddenly found himself as Zevon's manager. Slater went to work, pairing Zevon with R.E.M., an up-and-coming band formed by his old college pal Peter Buck, who were currently on a break, discouraged when their first two critically-acclaimed albums failed to find an audience. This high praise/low sales model was something Zevon was all too familiar with. The band – Zevon, Buck, Mike Mills and Bill Berry – demoed four new Zevon songs and played some shows as hindu love gods (Warren apparently only joined bands devoid of capital letters).

Saviour number two was Zevon himself, whose reignited passion for music blew away his initial cynicism. He wanted to give it another go, but when he looked in the mirror his own worst enemy was looking back, and his own worst enemy had an uncanny knack for burning bridges. He would only be taken seriously now if he were sober. It took a couple more years, but 19 March 1986 marked Zevon's first day of full sobriety, and then he hit the studio for the first time in half a decade.

Sentimental Hygiene is one of Zevon's best records, and a terrific way to announce to the world he was back. It would be inaccurate to proclaim it a return to form, as *The Envoy* was also a strong album, but there is a sense that Zevon decided to up his not-inconsiderable game. From the title track to 'Leave My Monkey Alone', this is a parade of top tunes. There might be a slight mellifluous dip during 'Detox Mansion', but Zevon is still deft lyrically, and the listener is on his side emotionally. Who doesn't want him to triumph over his awful, awful disease?

Writing in *Q*, Mark Cooper's opinion that *Sentimental Hygiene* was 'vintage Zevon contemporised by the tough-minded contributions of his mates', was representative of the positive reception the album received upon release. Bud Scoppa of *Creem* was more cautious. While full of praise for Zevon the lyricist – 'It's hard to imagine a more quotable album than this one' – Scoppa was less convinced by the musicality: reserving particular scorn for 'the stiff, stodgy rhythm section ... of R.E.M.', and Zevon's 'wobbly, monotone vocal delivery'.

Zevon's moment had come (again). The music press was in his corner. With R.E.M., he was backed by a critically-acclaimed and commercially successful alternative rock band who would go stratospheric upon the release of their album *Document*, released just two days after *Sentimental Hygiene*. In Virgin, he had a record label that believed in his talent and were willing to invest in him, as demonstrated by the album's $250,000 budget and the supporting videos. They also released a steady stream of six singles from the album, a strategy normally reserved for era-defining records such as *Thriller*, *Born in the U.S.A.*, and *Brothers in Arms*. And, of course, Warren brought a strong batch of songs to the table.

Sales-wise, the album peaked at 63 in *Billboard* during an eighteen-week run. This was 30 places higher than *The Envoy*, but still fell well short of record label expectations. *Sentimental Hygiene* was the first in a two-album contract, so the comeback was both on, and on shaky ground. Zevon's moment had come again, but whether he would be able to grab it, remained to be seen.

'Sentimental Hygiene' (Zevon)

The opening title track is a big, bold beast of a song that confidently proclaims, 'I'M BACK'. R.E.M.'s Peter Buck on guitar, Mike Mills on bass, and Bill Berry on drums support Zevon on most of the album, although Mills is missing on the opener, so Jorge Calderón steps into the breach. Another familiar face from the Asylum years is Waddy Wachtel, but despite this guitar power, it is Zevon's keyboards that dominate the verses, big arena riffs on a track that is otherwise indie in outlook.

Guitars come to the fore during the instrumental breaks, however, as Neil Young delivers not one but two paint-peeling solos, the second somehow out-scorching the blistering first. The narrator tells of how the routine can desolate the soul ('Every day I get up in the morning and go to work/And do my job... whatever'), and Young manages to evoke this bleakness while conjuring up an absolutely thrilling solo. It's an astonishingly generous cameo, the guitarist unselfishly providing a solo equal to anything he would produce for himself.

New label Virgin spent some money on a promotional video, Zevon's first since the 'Werewolves Of London' non-starter, and it enjoyed regular rotation on music cable network VH1. The clip was filmed in black and white, in keeping with the Herb Ritts cover art, and begins startlingly with a scrunched-up ear opening like a sped-up flower in time to Bill Berry's tub-thumping (*exactly* as odd as it sounds). There follows a montage of unconnected scenes and characters, strangely both nostalgic and timeless, interspersed with shots of Zevon lip-synching the lyrics. Apart from the exploding ear, it's not dissimilar to the video for 'Wonderful Life' by British singer-songwriter Black, released the same year.

And what exactly is sentimental hygiene? Zevon hadn't given it any thought, telling Sylvie Simmons of *Creem* that one of his jobs as a songwriter was 'trying to think of interesting phrases, and trying, whether deliberately or not, to make a lot of interpretations possible and a lot of meaning available to them'. Besides, he added, to invest the phrase with meaning would rob him of the pleasure of 'hearing all the weird explanations' others came up with.

'Boom Boom Mancini' (Zevon)

This is the second part of the sports trilogy that began with *Bad Luck Streak in Dancing School*'s 'Bill Lee', and which would conclude with the hockey-themed 'Hit Somebody!' from 2002's *My Ride's Here*.

A musical biography of boxer Ray Mancini, holder of the WBA lightweight title from 1982 to 1984, the rousing chorus focuses on Mancini's defence of his title against Bobby Chacon in January 1984, a fight that proved to be his final victory. Mancini's bouts with Alexis Arguello and Arturo Frias are referred to in the early verses, but the final verse unsurprisingly deals with the fight that led to one of boxing's greatest tragedies.

Mancini's fight against South Korean Duk-Koo Kim took place in Las Vegas on 13 November 1982. Most American commentators dismissed the Korean as a pushover, but despite taking a pummelling, Kim put up a brave and spirited performance, so much so that referee Richard Green felt unable to stop the fight. It was only when Kim hit the canvas in the fourteenth round that Green seized his opportunity to end the match. Kim briefly got back on his feet but soon collapsed, fell into a coma, and died five days later.

A devastated Mancini, who attended Kim's funeral in South Korea, subsequently wrestled with depression, and the tragedy was further compounded by the suicides of both Kim's mother and Green within months of Kim's death.

In the aftermath of the fight, changes were made to increase safety, the most significant being title fights reduced from fifteen to twelve rounds, and one wonders if this is one of the 'hypocrite judgements after the fact' that Zevon sneers about before concluding, 'The name of the game is be hit and hit back'. Is Zevon himself tilting at these safety-conscious windmills, or is he satirising those that tilt at them? The reportage nature of what Stephen King called 'One of the coldest appraisals of the sport of boxing ever written', suggests the former.

Musically, the song is as pugilistic as its subject matter, even tougher than the hard-bitten title track, and layered with dense, lumbering drumming from Bill Berry, and crunching, descending power chords during the second and fourth chorus lines. The song is structured around an ominous heavy metal framework at odds with the semi-celebratory nature of the 'Hurry on home' line, although the outro piano solo introduces a belated, lighter tone.

'The Factory' (Zevon)

The album tone lightens with 'The Factory', a fun slice of rockabilly in which Zevon does a *Born In The USA*-era Bruce Springsteen, the mid-song 'whoo-hoo-hoo-hooh' sounding uncannily Springsteen-esque, and lyrics like 'I was born in Mechanicsburg/My daddy worked for Pontiac 'til he got hurt' are unmistakably Bossy. But is Warren also doing a bit of a Zimmerman? The presence of Mr. Dylan on harmonica certainly strengthens that impression, his impassioned playing proving Bob to be every bit as unstinting in his generosity as Neil. Meanwhile, Zevon and Peter Buck provide acoustic and electric fretwork, respectively, counterbalancing Dylan's hobo harp beautifully.

'The Factory' possesses a spirit of fun and mischief that has led earlier critics to dismiss it as a novelty, but it's a little gem that allows the album to organically shift gears.

As a side note, and not that anyone's picking foxes from a tree, the lines 'Kickin' asbestos in the factory' and 'Breathin' that plastic in the factory' predict the mesothelioma that would eventually kill Zevon.

'Trouble Waiting To Happen' (J. D. Souther, Zevon)

This is overtly autobiographical and the first of three songs here where Zevon explores the tribulations of celebrity life, all-new terrain for the songwriter. The later tunes are mocking and satirical, but this, the first song written for the album, is therapy, an exercise in anger exorcism.

The second verse is the giveaway:

The mailman brought me the *Rolling Stone*
It said I was living at home alone
I read things I didn't know I'd done
It sounded like a lot of fun
I guess I've been bad or something

The latter lines are a trivial reference to Zevon's alcoholic blackouts (now genuinely a thing of the past), but the opening couplet, although also played down, unmistakeably alludes to Asylum Records' heartless dismissal of Zevon via *Rolling Stone*, and was written with J. D. Souther in the immediate aftermath.

The track is a lilting, mid-tempo bopper, with Berry again terrific behind the drum kit, and Zevon lays down a woozy, old-time rock and roll piano solo as the song heads for the fade. However, the star guests, former Stray Cat Brian Setzer and Zevon regular Don Henley, are ill-served by Niko Bolas' mixing of the album. Henley's harmonies are buried deep somewhere within the asthenosphere, and apart from an outburst of Duane Eddy-like twanging on the intro, Setzer appears to be playing one of those silent lead guitars you never read so much about.

'Reconsider Me' (Zevon)

Written in 1984, 'Reconsider Me' was first offered to Stevie Nicks via her then-producer and romantic partner Jimmy Iovine. She recorded it during the sessions for 1985's *Rock A Little*, even securing a co-writing credit, seemingly by singing some of the words in the wrong order, but it never made the final cut. It finally saw the light of day on her 1998 *Enchanted* box set.

'Reconsider Me' was later covered by notables such as The Pretenders and Steve Earle, but being another autobiographical piece, Zevon's take is unsurprisingly the song's sincerest reading. The person being asked to do the reconsidering was Crystal Zevon, but she declined the offer when, in his enthusiasm to play her the song, Warren totally blanked their daughter Ariel who'd been eagerly waiting to show her dad her report card and a picture she drew for him.

This is one of the album's two R.E.M.-free cuts, but it doesn't lack musical muscle, with Waddy Wachtel and Tom Petty and the Heartbreakers guitarist Mike Campbell on guitars, and longtime Peter Gabriel sideman Tony Levin slapping bass. Don Henley returns on harmonies, and while his vocals aren't as quiet as on the previous track, the mixing team really should've afforded him greater clarity. Both Wachtel and Henley had also contributed to the Stevie Nicks original.

'Reconsider Me', another fine example of Zevon balladry, served as the title track to a collection of Warren's love songs after his passing, presumably chosen in the hope people would do exactly that and discover that he was more than just 'that werewolf guy'.

'Detox Mansion' (Jorge Calderón, Zevon)

This is the second of the album's 'I'm a celebrity' songs and its third consecutive slice of autobiography. As the title suggests, it deals with Warren's experiences in rehab, but it also pokes sly fun at how receiving treatment for substance abuse became something of a you-know-you've-arrived moment, much as an appearance on *The Muppet Show* had been in the previous decade.

'Detox Mansion' received the bulk of attention upon the album's release and continues to do so in retrospective reviews, and it's easy to see why. First, it explains Zevon's five-year absence and celebrates his comeback, not just musically but personally, with his success in achieving sobriety. Secondly, it's full of whip-smart diary observations celebrating little victories, such as 'I've been rakin' leaves with Liza/Me and Liz clean up the yard' and 'We get therapy and lectures/We play golf in the afternoon'. One can almost see the wryly-arched eyebrow when Zevon later skewers the cynical detachment of celebrities who transform their need for urgent medical and psychological assistance into a potential cash cow ('I'm just dying to tell my story/For all my friends to read').

In their haste to praise the lyrics, no one thought to mention the tune, presumably because there isn't one. The verses are sung in the style of a chain gang without soul, the chorus is shouting by any other name, and the whole thing lacks melody. As discordant messes go, it's not bad, but it is *still* a discordant mess.

'Bad Karma' (Zevon)

Hail, hail, the gang's all here, as the full R.E.M. foursome reunites for this track, Michael Stipe popping in to provide backing vocals alongside Tom Petty timekeeper Stan Lynch. Added to this is David Lindley on bowed saz and Darius Degher (late of Darius and the Magnets, a band that fame forgot) on sitar, making 'Bad Karma' a wonderful exercise in musical eclecticism.

Despite the lyric's reliance on spiritual concepts such as karma and reincarnation, the song is simply another hymn of the hapless, a cosmic cousin of 'Poor Poor Pitiful Me'. The narrator might not be attempting suicide by lying down on a disused railway, but there's still a whiff of woe-is-me as he bemoans taking 'a wrong turn on the astral plane'.

Meanwhile, and as if in response to the thickly-trowelled dirge that preceded it, 'Bad Karma' has a melody and an infectiously catchy one at that; a couple of listens could lead to an outbreak of whistling. The lyric's Eastern elements are mirrored musically with some nice little arabesques, such as Degher's prominent sitar motifs in the chorus and Lindley's Turkish bowed saz at the coda, which is itself accompanied by Berry's appropriately evocative percussion. If a wrong turn was taken melody-wise on 'Detox Mansion', then 'Bad Karma' finds Zevon and company back on track.

'Even A Dog Can Shake Hands' (Peter Buck, Mike Mills, Bill Berry, Zevon)

From Hindu beliefs to the hindu love gods. This song is the only co-write from the Berry, Buck, Mills, and Zevon lineup that played a few shows under the love gods moniker in 1984, and is the concluding part of this album's 'celebrity' trilogy.

Zevon had his sights set on the music industry this time around and was obviously still smarting over the treatment he got from Asylum. Lines such as 'All the worms and the gnomes are having lunch at Le Dóme/They're living off the fat of the land' were unlikely to make him any new influential pals, but by this stage in his career, he was accustomed to the smell of those burning bridges.

The song is an up-tempo, heavy metal rockabilly with four, count 'em, four guitarists, Zevon and Buck being joined by Wachtel and Rick Richards of The Georgia Satellites. For all this firepower and an undeniable exuberance, the song is surprisingly restrained, though everyone sounds like they're having fun, not least Mr. Z., who whoops and hollers throughout. The song's only misstep is its premature fade, especially misjudged when one of the six-stringers had just begun to fly solo.

Appropriately, the song served as the theme to the 1999 US TV series *Action*, which was every bit irreverent and belligerent in skewering Hollywood. Though critically acclaimed, it ran for only one thirteen-episode season.

'The Heartache' (Zevon)

'Shadows falling in the afternoon/Blue feeling to the maximum'. What a wonderfully expressive, scene-setting opening couplet, put into brutal, heart-shattering context by the follow-up, 'Look what happens when you love someone/And they don't love you'. These lyrics touch all listeners because all listeners have lived them; in the days before conscious uncouplings, someone always got hurt when a relationship ended.

Sentimental Hygiene was Zevon's most guitar-driven album to date, so he knowingly changes tone here by leading with the keyboard, even going so far

Above: The Piano Fighter at the height of his late 1970s success.

Above: Sober of dress and sober of mind: Warren Zevon in the mid 1980s.

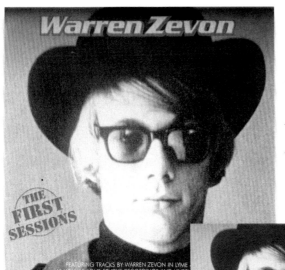

Left: Zevon's earliest work as part of lyme and cybelle was finally released on CD as *The First Sessions* in 2003, the year of his death. *(White Whale / Varése Sarabande)*

Right: stephen lyme and cybelle, aka Warren Zevon and Violet Santangelo, on the uncropped back cover of *The First Sessions*. *(White Whale / Varése Sarabande)*

LIKE THE SEASONS
(Lyme)

WW 244
(W144)
Ishmael Music
Inc. BMI
Time: 1:48

WHITE
WHALE

THE TURTLES
Produced by Bones Howe
for White Whale Records

WHITE WHALE RECORDS · 8961 SUNSET BOULEVARD · LOS ANGELES, CALIF.

Left: Zevon had many famous fans and supporters throughout his career, but The Turtles were there first, placing 'Like the Seasons' on the B-side of their million-selling single 'Happy Together'. *(White Whale)*

Right: The cover of Zevon's debut was shot by Robert Edlund, later part of the visual effects team that won an Academy Award for *Star Wars*. He received further nominations for his work on *Ghostbusters*, *Die Hard*, and *Alien 3*. *(EMI / Capitol)*

Above: 1976's *Warren Zevon*, a classic album about a Los Angeles far removed from that sung about by his Asylum Records labelmates. *(Asylum / Elektra)*

Left: Zevon and Browne perform 'Mohammed's Radio' on Britain's *The Old Grey Whistle Test*, December 1976.

Right: 'You better stay away from him; he'll rip your lungs out, Jim!'. Zevon in the 'Werewolves of London' promo video.

Left: Warren playing the Capitol Theatre, New Jersey on 1 October 1982 as part of *The Envoy* tour.

Right: The Capitol began life as a vaudeville theatre in 1921 and had a spell as an adult film theatre before becoming a popular rock venue in the 1970s and 1980s. Zevon's bassist on *The Envoy* tour was Larry Larson.

Left: Warren was a regular guest on David Letterman's shows from the 1980s on, even filling in for bandleader Paul Shaffer on several occasions. Here he is performing 'Splendid Isolation' in 1989.

Right: Zevon duets with Neil Young on 'Splendid Isolation' at the latter's seventh Bridge School Benefit in 1993. Young had supplied harmony vocals on the original recording.

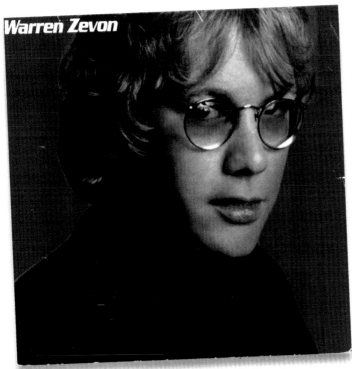

Left: *Excitable Boy* (1978). Zevon's only platinum-selling album was also his only top ten hit. Half of its songs became permanent fixtures on his setlist. *(Asylum / Rhino)*

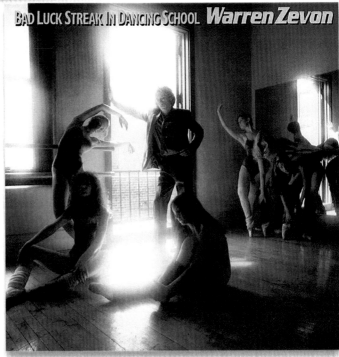

Right: The cover of 1980's *Bad Luck Streak in Dancing School* was shot by Jimmy Wachtel, as were all Zevon's album covers for his Asylum releases. *(Asylum / Elektra)*

Right: Wachtel had to defend the 'ballet and bullets' back cover of *Bad Luck Streak* after some women's groups had raised concerns about its implied violence. *(Asylum / Elektra)*

Left: After the commercial failure of 1982's *The Envoy*, Asylum terminated Zevon's contract. Zevon only discovered this by reading about it in *Rolling Stone*. *(Asylum / Rhino)*

Left: After a five-year hiatus, a newly clean and sober Zevon returns with a new record label, a new album, and a new backing band, R.E.M. *(Virgin)*

Right: Zevon succumbs to Eighties Day-Glo just as the decade draws to a close, but *Transverse City*'s eye-catching cover failed to catch many eyes and the album did not chart. *(Virgin)*

Right: The *Hindu Love Gods* album was a drunken bit of fun recorded by Zevon, Peter Buck, Mike Mills and Bill Berry during the *Sentimental Hygiene* sessions. Its release three years later caused a rift between R.E.M. and Zevon. *(Giant / Reprise)*

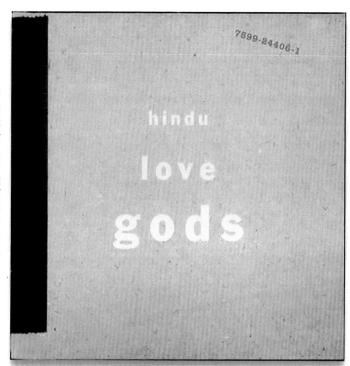

Left: A new label, a new record, a new set of top tunes, the same old song. *Mr. Bad Example* troubled no charts, and a disappointed Zevon must have been left wondering what a guy had to do to catch a break. *(Giant / Reprise)*

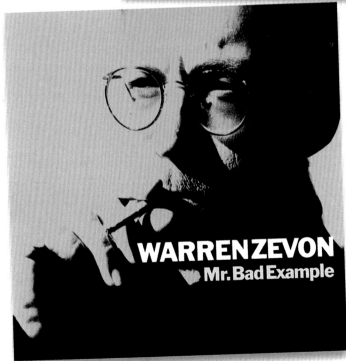

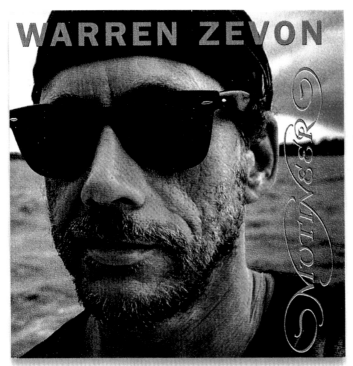

Left: 1995's *Mutineer* was reportedly the lowest-selling album of Zevon's career. Its failure led to another five-year break from the industry. *(Giant)*

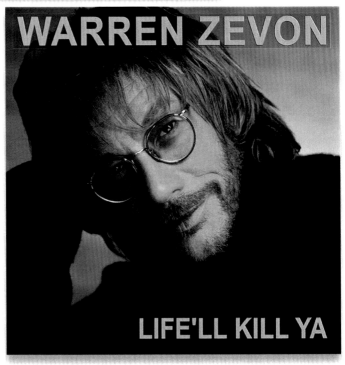

Right: Zevon bounced back with the critically revered *Life'll Kill Ya*, the first of three albums on the Artemis label with death as a central theme. Back in 2000, no one saw the punchline coming. *(Artemis)*

Right: More unplanned prescience: The car Zevon peers out from on the cover of *My Ride's Here* (2002) is a hearse. He would be diagnosed with terminal cancer within months of this album's release. *(Artemis)*

Left: *The Wind* (2003) was Zevon's star-studded swan song, giving him his first top 20 hit since *Excitable Boy* twenty-five years previously. Zevon died less than two weeks after its 26 August release. *(Artemis)*

Left: Warren, playing himself, hits on Susan (Brooke Shields) in a 1999 episode of *Suddenly Susan*.

Right: With musician-actor Rick Springfield, in the same episode of *Suddenly Susan*.

Left: A still from the promotional video for 'Keep Me in Your Heart', the last song Zevon recorded.

Right: A press ad for Zevon's UK tour in 2000. This was Warren's first British tour since 1976, although he did play London in 1988 and 1992. *(Photograph by Joshua Gallagher)*

Left: The 'dirty John Denver' plays the BBC's *Later .... With Jools Holland* show, May 2000.

Right: Lee Ho Fook, the restaurant named in 'Werewolves of London', was a real place. It is now an eatery called Dumplings' Legend, and big dishes of beef chow mein are no longer on the menu. *(Photograph by Joshua Gallagher)*

Left: *A Quiet Normal Life* anthologises Zevon's Asylum years, with half its fourteen tracks lifted from *Excitable Boy*. *(Asylum / Elektra)*

warren zevon preludes

Right: The 2007 release *Preludes: Rare and Unreleased Recordings* unearthed some buried treasure recorded prior to the release of *Warren Zevon* in 1976. It was released on vinyl for Record Store Day 2021. *(New West Records)*

and unreleased recordings

'ENJOY EVERY SANDWICH'
THE SONGS OF
WARREN ZEVON

performed by

JACKSON BROWNE
with BONNIE RAITT

JORGE CALDERÓN
and JENNIFER WARNES

BOB DYLAN

STEVE EARLE
and RECKLESS KELLY

DON HENLEY

DAVID LINDLEY
and RY COODER

PIXIES

ADAM SANDLER

JILL SOBULE

BRUCE SPRINGSTEEN

BILLY BOB THORNTON

THE WALLFLOWERS

PETE YORN

and

JORDAN ZEVON

Left: *Enjoy Every Sandwich: The Songs of Warren Zevon,* an all-star tribute to Zevon released a year after his passing, featured big guns such as Bob Dylan and Bruce Springsteen. *(Artemis)*

Right: Zevon's scorching live album *Stand in the Fire* only reached 80 on the *Billboard* chart, sixty places lower than its predecessor. The singer retained critical acclaim for the rest of his career, but as far as Joe Public was concerned, his fifteen minutes were up. *(Asylum/Rhino)*

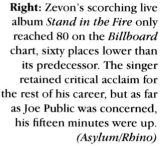

Left: *Learning to Flinch* featured the singer playing solo. Its approach may have chimed with the spate of then-current *MTV Unplugged* albums, but it was made with an eye on the budget rather than the latest trend. *(Giant)*

Right: *I'll Sleep When I'm Dead: An Anthology* comprises material from the Asylum, Virgin, and Giant years, and is the most comprehensive collection of Zevon's work to date. *(Rhino)*

Left: Zevon made his final public appearance on the *Late Show with David Letterman* on 30 October 2002. He called his host 'the best friend my music's ever had'.

Right: The cover of Crystal Zevon's oral biography, *I'll Sleep When I'm Dead*. Crystal was unsparing with her punches at the request of her former husband. *(HarperCollins; front cover photograph by Jimmy Wachtel)*

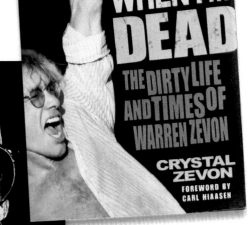

Left: 'Old Velvet Nose' appeared on the back cover of every album from *Mr. Bad Example* onwards. Zevon claimed it reminded him to 'lighten up a little bit' before it was too late.

as to include a solo, one reminiscent of an Old West folk song via the Celtic diaspora. Like backing vocalists on previous tracks, Jennifer Warnes is arguably too low in the mix, but here it works, her presence the lingering ghost of the person that walked out.

'The Heartache' is another of Zevon's seemingly effortless supreme ballads, probably superior to 'Reconsider Me'. It's one of life's baffling little mysteries that it has never been anthologised or covered.

'Leave My Monkey Alone' (Zevon)

Warren had been so busy with his shiny new slagging-the-celebrity-lifestyle song cycle that he nearly forgot to throw in one of his classic historical geopolitical cocktails, but fortunately, here's 'Leave My Monkey Alone' to fit that particular bill.

This is Zevon's most funky off-the-beaten track since *Excitable Boy*'s 'Nighttime In The Switching Yard', and with R.E.M. presumably on the midnight train back to Georgia, Warren turns to Parliament-Funkadelic alumni Blackbyrd McKnight and Amp Fiddler for assistance, even managing to draft the Father of the House himself, George Clinton, to arrange the track. Further musical muscle is supplied by Flea of the Red Hot Chilli Peppers (miscredited as 'Flee'). It will perhaps surprise no one to learn that it's a much more satisfying effort than 1978's funk flop, although the end of British colonial rule in Africa sounds about as implausible a dance lyric as the earlier one about trains. Maybe this was Zevon's failed attempt to make clubbing more highbrow.

This song was released as a single, and Virgin again stumped up the money for a video, this time starring Clinton, Zevon, and an ill-advised hat in an arresting hybrid of Peter Gabriel's 'Sledgehammer', a-ha's 'Take On Me', and some of Paul Simon's more quirky *Graceland* videos. With just a little airplay and a whole lot of luck, it might just have made it, much like the equally off-kilter single 'Walk the Dinosaur' by Was Not Was did the same year. But alas, that all-important airplay / luck combo was not forthcoming.

For those that are counting, this is Zevon's third ape song, after 'Gorilla' and 'Gorilla, You're a Desperado'.

Transverse City (1989)

Personnel:
Warren Zevon: vocals, keyboards, guitar, harmonica
Bob Glaub: bass
Richie Hayward: drums
Neil Young: lead guitar on 'Gridlock'; harmony on 'Splendid Isolation'
Jerry Garcia: guitar on 'Transverse City' and 'They Moved The Moon'
David Gilmour: guitar on 'Run Straight Down'
Waddy Wachtel: guitars on 'Run Straight Down', 'Networking', and 'Nobody's In Love This Year'
Chick Corea: piano on 'The Long Arm Of The Law'
Jack Casady: bass on 'They Moved The Moon' and 'Gridlock'
Mike Campbell: guitar on 'Splendid Isolation'; guitar and mandolin on 'Nobody's In Love This Year'
Benmont Tench: organ on 'Networking'
Jorge Calderón: bass on 'Networking'
Howie Epstein: banjo and mandolin on 'Networking'; bass on 'Down In The Mall'
Jorma Kaukonen: acoustic guitar on 'Gridlock'
David Lindley: lap steel and saz on 'Down In The Mall'
Mark Isham: flugelhorn on 'Nobody's In Love This Year'
Rob Jaczko: percussion
Producers: Warren Zevon, Duncan Aldrich, Andrew Slater
Recorded at Mad Hatter Studios and A&M Studios, Los Angeles; Red Zone Studios, Burbank; Broken Arrow Ranch, California; Abbey Road Studios, London; Paisley Park Studios, Chanhassen, Minnesota
Release date: October 1989
Label: Virgin
Chart Placing: US: Did not chart
Running time: 41:40

It may not have hit the hoped-for heights, but *Sentimental Hygiene* had nudged Zevon's career in the right direction. It would be natural for him to pick up where he left off and pen a clutch of hard-rocking songs that genetically mapped his polished L.A.-noir to the prevalent indie aesthetic, but 'woozy from reading the Thomas Pynchon canon at a sitting', he opted instead for that least fashionable of musical statements, the concept album. Zevon had also fallen under the spell of William Gibson's *Neuromancer*, a novel that, despite its futuristic trappings, was seen as 'a poetic evocation of life in the late-1980s rather than as science fiction'. Zevon conceived an album that would do precisely the same, one whose subject matter would be all that was wrong in the world, or soon would be. With added entropy. One can all but see Richard Branson and his Virgin chums punching the air in unfettered delight.

Transverse City is a disc-shaped dichotomy. On one hand, it has two of Zevon's best songs, the joyous energy burst of 'Splendid Isolation' and the spellbinding 'Nobody's In Love This Year', each essential to casual fan and committed Zevonista alike. On the other hand, there's no escaping that this is the weakest of Warren's major-label releases. Each of his previous albums contained a questionable track, but here the quotient is doubled thanks to the going-nowhere-slow title cut and the equally lumbering 'They Moved The Moon'. The remaining songs lie on a spectrum between these two points.

The reviews were similarly mixed upon the album's release. Edward Pouncy of *New Musical Express* – who praised *Sentimental Hygiene* as 'a magnificent return to form' and 'one of the year's great records' – thought *Transverse City* was 'simply not the well-greased machine gun of a record that Warren Zevon usually pulls out of his kit bag'.

Zevon's decreasing fan base agreed, and decreased further. Despite two strong singles receiving airplay that punched way above Zevon's usual quota, and a video for 'Run Straight Down' that enjoyed a spell on VH1, the album stiffed, his greatest commercial flop since 1969's unloved *Wanted Dead or Alive*. Zevon's two-record contract with Virgin was now over, and they chose not to renew.

'Transverse City' (Stefan Arngrim, Zevon)

Here's the song of shear and torsion
Here's the bloodbath magazine
Here's the harvest of contusions
Here's the narcoleptic dream

Words as esoteric as this, remind this reviewer, then and now, that no one else was writing songs like this, and that, then and now, this reviewer doesn't have a clue what it means.

This 'song of shear and torsion' is essentially a litany of phrases culled from Zevon's recent reading habits and *Scientific American*, as it casually name-checks 'the endless neon vistas', 'the shiny, mylar towers', and 'the all-night trauma stand'. Zevon's lyrical adroitness has been rightly praised by many a critic, but here he tips from being clever into being too clever by far. What he is written sounds as if it might be interesting, but it is never engaging.

'Transverse City' also suffers from a lack of discernible melody. It all starts well enough, Zevon's synth and jazz bassist John Patitucci conjuring up some exotic Asian locale. Little Feat drummer Richie Hayward joining in also serves as Zevon's cue to sing, and sing he does, in a droning monotone that doesn't let up till the end of this chorus-free, dirge-like anti-ditty. The Grateful Dead's Jerry Garcia is in there too, giving his all, his guitar solo striking out on its own hippie trail, but even the head Deadhead can't inject life into this one.

The song's co-writer was Canadian actor Stefan Arngrim, best remembered for playing Barry Lockridge in the late 1960s TV series *Land of the Giants*. At the time of recording *Transverse City*, he was Warren's AA sponsor. According to Arngrim, Warren produced four demos for his band Knights of the Living Dead during these sessions.

'Run Straight Down' (Zevon)

Does any lyric scream '1980s' quite as much as 'Fluorocarbons in the ozone layer/First the water and the wildlife go'? It's fair to say this was a pretty big thing back then. The ozone layer's offending hole was discovered on 16 May 1985, and it was, to put it mildly, a bit of a worry. Thankfully, the 1987 Montreal Protocol – signed by 197 countries and the only UN treaty to achieve universal ratification – led to a significant decline in ozone-depleting gasses in the atmosphere. 'We didn't start the fire', said Billy Joel the same year 'Run Straight Down' was released as a single, but he was misinformed; we totally did, but for once, we got together to put it out.

Warren's still Mr. Glass Half-Empty, but at least now, the gloom comes with a tune. The song opens with a Gregorian chant of things that don't sound at all healthy (4-aminobyphenyl, a carcinogenic that causes bladder cancer; hexachlorobenzene, a fungicide banned globally by the Stockholm Convention on Persistent Organic Pollutants), while studio effects give the impression that the track was recorded in a dynamo. A very English guitar solo twists and bends throughout, and if it calls to mind, for example, 'Comfortably Numb', that's because Zevon's dipped into his little red book and enlisted Pink Floyd's Dave Gilmour. J. D. Souther gets a better production deal than his Mellow Mafia associates on the previous album, and offers effective harmonies. Altogether it's a step up from the title cut, and would've made for a superior album opener.

Virgin financed another video, all post-Chernobyl paranoia via 1930s Universal monster flicks, with Gilmour in a co-starring role. It helped propel the song to number 30 on the *Billboard* mainstream rock chart.

'The Long Arm Of The Law' (Zevon)

This starts promisingly enough, Zevon laying down an atmospheric keyboard wash, with Bob Glaub and Richie Hayward keeping it understated but interesting. Chick Corea drops in with some nimble and suitable jazz piano before the whole thing morphs into a poorly aged but pleasing set-piece driven by Zevon's still-dreaming-of-arenas guitar and keyboard riffing. Warren then opens the song with the nice cliché-smashing line, 'When I was young, times were hard/When I got older it was worse'.

All in all, this song has a wonderfully crafted setup but ultimately fails to deliver. With songs like 'Lawyers, Guns and Money', Zevon could tell a story with broadly sketched pithiness, but that talent deserts him here, leaving the lyrics quite fragmentary. There's something about a 1999 war in Paraguay, and a hint of some illegal activity – gunrunning perhaps – but the ideas remain precisely that. It doesn't help that the verses always seem to sprint for the chorus, either. Coincidentally, Warren's son Jordan sings harmony vocals here, for the first time since 1982's 'The Hula Hula Boys', where his Hawaiian lyric translated loosely as 'get to the chorus', advice this song takes too much to heart.

In the end, it's not the worst song in the Zevon canon, but it's unlikely to crack anyone's personal top 10. It's biggest sin, however, is it takes a player of Chick Corea's stature and stereotypes his genre. In the first instrumental break, an absonant mess, all four players seem to be playing completely different songs, apparently because that's jazz, man!

'Turbulence' (Zevon)
Things pick up considerably with 'Turbulence', a song chronicling the dying days of the Soviet Union from the perspective of a conscripted soldier, who, like many of the working class everywhere, laments how the decisions of distant politicians can impact on him.

The speculative fiction of 'The Long Arm of the Law' is superseded by the news of the day, albeit from a Russian point of view. The narrator name-checks the Soviet Union's last leader Mikhail Gorbachev and perestroika, his program of political and economic reforms and another buzzword of the decade, and Eduard Shevardnadze, the Soviet Minister of Foreign Affairs who played a key role in ending the Cold War. Gorbachev and Shevardnadze were a new breed of Russian politician, much-praised by the West, but it is 'same as it ever was' for the poor soldier that finds himself drafted to Afghanistan to take on the mujahideen. Zevon nods to his East Slavic heritage by singing a refrain in Russian, in which, according to translations offered on various lyric websites, our hero is surrounded by enemies and wanting his mama. 'Turbulence' has a similar word count to its predecessor, but the lyrics are more cohesive, resulting in a complete story song, deftly told.

Musically it's a blast, with just Zevon, Glaub and Hayward comprising the studio band, Souther returning on harmony vocal duties. Glaub and Hayward provide rhythm for half the album's songs, and are excellent throughout, but it's here on a song free from celebrity guests that they really shine. Their playing is always inventive but never flashy, serving the song perfectly, sitting tight behind Zevon's guitar and keys. Between them, the trio cut a power-pop classic, Hayward even contributing a faint cowbell during the fade. Or maybe it was a Moscowbell.

'They Moved The Moon' (Zevon)
This song has a nice synthesizer strings intro, reminiscent of the interludes that peppered *Bad Luck Streak In Dancing School*. It has a nice solo, which leads into an equally nice vocal refrain. The backing track could provide a John Carpenter film with a nice soundtrack. But none of these things are nice enough to prevent this song from being a plodding, mind-numbing, doom-laden threnody. This track makes the title cut sound like a delectable slice of sunshine pop.

Jerry Garcia is back on guitar, or so the credits inform us, but it would take a keen ear to pick out his guitar amongst Zevon's droning synths and naive drum patterns, and while the plump bass of Jefferson Airplane / Hot Tuna alumni Jack Casady lets its individuality be known, it is so simplistic that it too might as well have been pre-programmed.

'Splendid Isolation' (Zevon)

This track – its title derived from the nineteenth-century British foreign policy of avoiding permanent alliances – arrives with an echo-laden snare drum, followed by a giddy, harmonica-heavy sugar rush of an introduction. The hangover of disappointment caused by the previous song is instantly and gloriously blown away.

Glaub and Hayward return, as effortlessly accomplished as ever, and the guests include Heartbreaker Mike Campbell on guitar and Neil Young on unmistakable nasal whine. But it is Zevon who steals the show, highly capable on guitar, outstanding on harmonica, and simply stellar on piano. Indeed, 'Splendid Isolation' might be the best piano performance of Zevon's recording career, dense and ornate, full of surprising frills and memorable arpeggios, totally dominating and driving the song. It's a life-affirming piece of music, better experienced than described.

The lyrics are true to the title, describing examples of isolation so splendid only the rich and famous can afford it, whether it be Georgia O'Keeffe retreating to her New Mexico ranch or Michael Jackson buying private access to Disneyland. The last verse presents an unnerving alternative, where the celebrity is stalked by their fans, and resorts to putting 'tinfoil up on the windows/Lying down in the dark to dream' because they 'don't want to see their faces' and they 'don't want to hear them scream'. In these lines, Zevon realises the nightmarish potential that accompanies a level of fame he could only dream about.

Virgin released 'Splendid Isolation' as the album's second single, but, bafflingly, it never troubled any listings, not even the *Billboard* mainstream rock chart. If a song so irrepressibly catchy and joyful couldn't make it, one had to wonder whether Zevon would ever catch a break again. Public indifference notwithstanding, 'Splendid Isolation' remains one of his very best songs.

'Networking' (Arngrim, Zevon)

'Networking' is a three-minute slab of happy pop that has fun playing with the then-current computer lexicon:

Networking, I'm user-friendly
Networking I install with ease
Data processed, truly basic
I will upload you, you can download me

Zevon is on keyboards and Wachtel back on guitar, but it is two Heartbreakers that really make their mark. Howie Epstein's mandolin and, especially, banjo all but play the role of rhythm guitar, while Benmont Tench lays down a psychedelic swirl that wouldn't have been out of place two decades earlier. These choices may seem at odds with a song about cutting-edge technology, but it ultimately proved to be more forward-thinking than just draping the melody in synths or computer noises, as 'Networking' sounds as fresh now as the day it was cut. That said, Zevon does use synthesizers to simulate a lively brass section, and gives the song additional punch.

'Gridlock' (Zevon)
While watching Neil Young lay down his guitar lead for 'Sentimental Hygiene', Warren, with mouth agape, mused, 'This is like Woodstock, man!'. So how excited must he have been when recording 'Gridlock', which featured three Yasgur's Farm veterans in the shape of Young (lead guitar) and former Jefferson Airplane members Jorma Kaukonen and Jack Casady (acoustic guitar and bass, respectively). Throw in Little Feat's Richie Hayward and Zevon himself, and you have a veritable West Coast supergroup.

Appropriately for a song about traffic, Zevon shifts gears, the pop of 'Networking' morphing into a slow heavy-metal crawl indicative of the congestion described.

The lyric works because every driver can relate to the situation, and because Zevon tells his story well. The scene is well-described – 'The paramedics and the CHP/Wait impatiently for catastrophes' – as is the narrator's growing frustration: 'It's 5:00 p.m. on a weekday, friend/I'm going home, but I don't know when'. Of note is the last verse line, 'I feel like going on a killing spree', which acknowledges *road rage*, a relatively new phenomenon that would become an all-too-common societal blight the following decade.

'Gridlock' is a mid-table song, with a surprising pastoral folky mid-section that serves as an oasis of calm amidst the crunching chords, and a punky-glam chorus of 'Hey! Hey!' towards the end. It is an inoffensive, not entirely unpleasing filler, but is certainly unworthy of the august assemblage gathered to play on it.

'Down In The Mall' (Zevon)
The hard-rocking continues, with Zevon taking a caustic pop at consumerism. It's not a new target, and bands like The Clash, The Slits, X-Ray Spex and Devo skewered it particularly well in the post-punk era, so Warren wisely opts not for cynicism or social commentary but simply holds a mirror up and asks if you see anyone you know. And who doesn't recognise themselves in lyrics like 'We'll shop up a storm till we can't shop anymore/Then we're stopping off at the video store'? The only thing missing is the Chinese takeaway.

And then there's the neat couplet, 'We're buying CDs, and we're buying lingerie/We'll put it on a charge account we're never gonna pay', which acutely observes not only the 'American approach' to credit, but also the inevitable shopping drift: you go to the mall with your partner and end up going to the shops you would go to if you were on your own anyway.

It's a four-man celebrity-free band this time around, with Zevon and Hayward joined by Howie Epstein, David Lindley with his faithful lap steel, an oud and a saz for a dash of exotica. But despite the maestro's presence, it is Zevon's guitar-playing that grabs the spotlight. From the snarling intro to the extended fade-out solo (one of his best), his playing is exemplary, adding bite to and somewhat elevating a second successive mid-table song.

'Nobody's In Love This Year' (Zevon)

Zevon's skill at penning exquisite ballads has already been established, but here he takes it to dazzling new heights. A ballad of such grace might initially seem a poor fit considering the rest of the album's content, but it's another perfect snapshot of late-20th-century life in America, this time centred on the increasing friends-with-benefits and open-relationship trends. 'I don't want to be Mr. Vulnerable', sings Zevon at his most soulful. 'I don't want to be the one who gets left behind'. There's no sarcasm or bitterness here, just a cautionary note. It sounds suspiciously like he sings from experience, as if burnt by recent relationships and no longer wanting to play with fire. Not coincidentally, his brief romance with Annette Aguilar, whom he met at an AA meeting, had recently ended, much to Warren's dismay. She was also the inspiration for 'Searching For A Heart', which would appear on his next solo album.

It doesn't hurt that he surrounds himself with masters of their craft, here exemplified by Mike Campbell's delicate mandolin, Wachtel's brightly chiming rhythm guitar, and the ever-dependable Glaub and Hayward (the latter sensational with his understated drumming, particularly the dramatic return to play after falling silent during the chorus). But what makes the hairs stand on end is the ethereal flugelhorn, played by film composer Mark Isham, that flutters on butterfly wings about Zevon's world-weary vocal, giving a beautiful juxtaposition of air and weight. 'Nobody's In Love This Year' is simply gorgeous.

Hindu Love Gods (1990)

Personnel:
Warren Zevon: vocals, guitar
Peter Buck: guitar
Mike Mills: bass
Bill Berry: drums
Producers: Andrew Slater, Niko Bolas
Recorded at Record One, Sherman Oaks; A&M Studios, Los Angeles
Release date: 5 October 1990
Label: Giant/Reprise/Warner Bros.
Chart placing: US: 168
Running time: 36:58

When interviewed by Nick Hasted of *The Independent* in 1989 after the failure of *Transverse City*, Zevon was philosophical, comparing what he did for a living, not to other rock stars, but to 'real people doing their jobs as best they can'. With that as his benchmark, he didn't think in terms of record sales, but rather his good fortune in making his living as a musician: 'As early as I can remember, I had this sense that I would be an artist, a fine artist as opposed to a pop artist. And as such, I assumed that I would survive and be content with that. I did, and I am'.

Zevon's serenity under the circumstances is commendable, but he did have a manager in Andy Slater, and Slater's primary job now was to secure his client a new record contract. Fortunately, he had a cunning plan. One of Zevon's former managers, industry legend Irving Azoff, had just launched Giant Records, and Slater wanted Azoff to sign his client to the fledgling label. Azoff had a fondness for Zevon, but, recalling his wayward ways, perhaps also a wariness. Anticipating hesitation on Azoff's part, Slater came armed with a deal sweetener.

Three years earlier, Zevon had leftover studio time upon completing *Sentimental Hygiene*. Just for kicks, he and his core backing band of R.E.M. decided to run through some blues standards, with a couple of recent hits – Prince's 'Raspberry Beret', and a song made famous by The Georgia Satellites, 'Battleship Chains' – thrown in for good measure. Bill Berry told Andy Gill of *Q*: 'It took about as long to do as it takes to listen to it. Warren would go, "It's in E, here's the tempo. When I shake my head like this, we'll stop". It was all done first or second take'.

The songs were recorded for posterity but were never meant for commercial release, not least because the R.E.M. players were inebriated during the session (Warren maintained his sobriety). Zevon took his tape of the session, titled it *Monkey Wash, Donkey Rinse*, played it a few times in his car, and then left it on the shelf. He also gave a copy to Slater.

R.E.M. had become major stars since the recording of *Sentimental Hygiene*, scoring platinum-selling albums in *Document* and *Green,* and hitting the US top-10 with 'The One I Love' and 'Stand'. With that in mind, Slater offered Azoff *Monkey Wash, Donkey Rinse*. The acclaimed, nigh-on legendary singer-songwriter backed by America's hottest new(ish) band? This, surely, was a winner. Azoff agreed, signed Zevon, and released the session as *hindu love gods*.

While the Zevon/R.E.M. conglomerate might initially sound enticing, the throwaway nature of the recording sessions relegates *hindu love gods* to the least essential album in the Zevon canon. There are some good cuts in the shape of 'Junko Pardner', 'Raspberry Beret' and a couple of others, but these are strictly good, as opposed to essential, while at least half the album need never trouble the ear canals again.

The album's appearance in October 1990 came as an unwelcome surprise to the R.E.M. camp, who hadn't been informed that their drunken whimsy of three years ago was now in record stores. Even worse, Andy Slater was trying to cajole them into joining Zevon in promoting the album and the 'Raspberry Beret' single. R.E.M., on the cusp of releasing their soon-to-be mega-selling and Grammy-winning *Out of Time* album, understandably could see the whole thing far enough, and certainly didn't appreciate accusations of sabotaging Zevon's career.

Meanwhile, Zevon actively promoted the record, giving interviews to the music press and performing on *Late Night with David Letterman*. In a 1995 interview with *Goldmine*'s Steve Roesser, Zevon expressed a degree of remorse about the album, and openly blamed Slater for the fiasco, saying, 'I told my manager, "This is all yours. I don't want to see it, I don't want to argue about it, I don't want to hear about it. Whatever you want, whatever you're gonna do, it's up to you"'. That contrition, such as it was, proved to be short-lived, as 'Raspberry Beret' was included on the following year's *I'll Sleep When I'm Dead* anthology, and 2002's *Genius: The Best of Warren Zevon*. These might have been decisions made by the record company rather than the artist, but once more, the air was thick with the stench of burning bridges.

'Walkin' Blues' (Robert Johnson)

The credits cite Robert Johnson as the composer of 'Walkin' Blues', but it was actually written by Son House, with Johnson later adapting it. Both versions have primitive acoustic arrangements, which Zevon and company wisely sidestep, offering instead, an urgent electric take with frantic percussive downstrokes. Ultimately, it sounds less like the Mississippi Delta, and more like the sound of Canvey Island, home of veteran UK rhythm 'n' bloozers Dr. Feelgood.

'Travelin' Riverside Blues' (Johnson)

This time it *is* a Robert Johnson song, and again, the gods come across like a convincing Dr. Feelgood tribute band, with some fine sloppy drumming from Bill Berry. Is this deliberate, or is it simply the likely outcome when the blues and the booze are added to guitar, bass and drums? Whereas Zevon demonstrated real rock-and-roll singing chops on the opener, here he's more faithful to the Johnson original, strangulated words and all.

'Raspberry Beret' (Prince)

This version pooh-poohs the intricacies of the original, dropping a bridge and verse for good measure, opting for loud and raucous instead. By putting their own stamp on it, the hindu love gods follow what should be the golden rule of cover versions: respect the original but don't regurgitate it. This was the track that got the most attention, which is the probable outcome 99 per cent of the time you drop a Prince song in amongst old blues standards that even your band don't know. It reached 23 on the US Modern Rock chart.

'Crosscut Saw' (Fred Ingrahm, Bill Sanders)

According to Gerard Herzhaft writing in his *Encyclopaedia of the Blues*, Albert King's 1966 version of 'Crosscut Saw' 'made it one of the necessary pieces of modern blues'. Backed by Booker T. & the MG's, and featuring an effortlessly cool brass section, King's take is worth checking out. However, if you are one of those that think all blues sounds the same, give the hindu love gods version a spin and feel absolutely vindicated.

Again, the authorship listed above is as per the album credits and should be taken with a bucket of salt.

'Junko Pardner' (Bob Shad)

This song has been recorded by a wide range of artists, including Louis Jordan, Dr. John, The Clash and Hugh Lawrie. One might think Zevon would remember the lyrics of such a well-read song, but nope, he manages a couple of verses and then substitutes extra choruses in lieu of the rest. He even spells the title wrong ('Junko' instead of 'Junco'). We can forgive him, however, as he and the band are clearly having a hoot, giving this old chestnut its liveliest ever reading. 'Junko Pardner' is that most contradictory of beasts, a blues song that's fun. If the previous song upheld preconceived notions about the genre, prepare to have them smashed here.

'Mannish Boy' (Bo Diddley, Melvin London, Muddy Waters)

Dah-Duh-Da-Duh! Here's 'Mannish Boy' with what must be the blues' most iconic, parodied, and overplayed riff, although it almost certainly predates Muddy Waters' 1955 release. Waters rerecorded it in 1977, with Johnny Winters providing some background hoots and huzzahs. This po-faced hindu love gods run-through could do with some of that fake excitement.

'Wang Dang Doodle' (Willie Dixon)

This much covered Willie Dixon standard always had a kick-the-shit rhythm, but here it's given some added spikiness. Zevon would be the first to admit he's no Little Walter but lays down some convincing blues harp anyway. That said, the exhilaration that sold 'Walkin' Blues' and 'Junko Pardner' is totally lacking here.

'Battleship Chains' (Terry Anderson)

Here hindu love gods forget the golden rule of cover songs and offer up a slavish bar band version of 'Battleship Chains', originally by The Woods but made famous by The Georgia Satellites. It's not bad, but that's down to the tune's pre-existing catchiness more than anything Zevon and company bring to the table.

'I'm A One-Woman Man' (Tillman Franks, Johnny Horton)

This Johnny Horton country hit is treated like a novelty song, with Zevon channelling his inner Gabby Hayes and singing as if gurning throughout. Perhaps he adopted this approach because he knew the title certainly didn't apply to him. Totally forgettable.

'Vigilante Man' (Woody Guthrie)

The delivery of 'Vigilante Man' has always bordered on the torturous, be it the Guthrie original or the later covers by Ry Cooder or Nazareth. The hindu love gods give it a wide-screen western makeover, injecting some much-needed life into this hoariest of dust bowl ballads, making their reading one of the song's finest renditions.

Related songs:
'Gonna Have A Good Time Tonight' (George Young, Harry Vanda)

This was the first Zevon, Berry, Buck and Mills recording released under the hindu love gods banner, with R.E.M.-associate Bryan Cook on keyboards and vocals. This single, a cover of the Easybeats song 'Good Times', was recorded in 1984 and issued two years later on R.E.M.'s label I.R.S.. A planned recording rather than a studio whim, it's a more polished affair than the later album, with Zevon pulling a pretty good Mick Jagger impersonation.

'Narrator' (Bill Berry)

The B-side of 'Gonna Have A Good Time Tonight' was a Bill Berry composition that R.E.M. played live but never recorded. It doesn't include Zevon.

Mr. Bad Example (Giant, 1991)

Personnel:
Warren Zevon: vocals, keyboards, guitar
Waddy Wachtel: guitar
Bob Glaub: bass
Jeff Porcaro: drums
Dan Dugmore: guitar on 'Model Citizen'; pedal steel on 'Heartache Spoken Here'
Jorge Calderón: bass on 'Mr. Bad Example'
Jim Keltner: drums on 'Things To Do in Denver When You're Dead'; additional
drums on 'Mr Bad Example'
David Lindley: fiddle on 'Renegade'; lap steel, saz and cumbus on 'Quite Ugly One
Morning'
Harmony vocals: Waddy Wachtel, Jordan Zevon, Tito Larriva, Jorge Calderón,
Dwight Yoakam, Michael Lennon, Mark Lennon, Kip Lennon,Warren Zevon
Producer: Waddy Wachtel
Recorded at The Sound Factory, Los Angeles; Dodge City, Glendale, CA
Release date: 15 October 1991
Label: Giant
Chart placing: Did not chart
Running time: 40:15

Andy Slater may have been made the villain in the *hindu love gods* debacle,
but at the end of the day, he was doing his job – getting his client exposure,
a record deal, and into the Modern Rock chart. From the start, he had been
tireless, preventing Frontline Management from dropping Warren, hooking
him up with R.E.M., restoking his interest in playing live, getting him back into
the studio, and, crucially, getting him signed to Virgin America, and, when they
dropped him, securing a deal with Irving Azoff's fledgling Giant Records. Slater
had also been there for Warren on a personal level, lending him money, taking
him to rehab, helping with his sobriety, and – less honourably – once talking
a young woman Zevon had got pregnant, into having an abortion. However, if
Slater thought any of this bought him loyalty, he was wrong.

In Crystal Zevon's biography, Slater recounts how he himself was in rehab
when he got a call from his client, who said, 'Look, Andy, I just got off the
phone with Irving. He says that if I fire you and make a change in management,
he'll really work my record ... Listen, man, I'm 44 years old, and this is my last
chance. I'm sorry'.

Warren's contract was picked up by Peter Asher, a former 1960s hitmaker
with Peter and Gordon and Linda Ronstadt's manager for much of her career,
although the day-to-day management would fall to Gloria Boyce.

Meanwhile, Zevon found a new addiction to compensate for drink and
drugs being off the table: sex. He was never single, and rarely monogamous.
A scorecard would not be unhelpful. One minute he's with *Rolling Stone*
journalist Merle Ginsberg, then performance artist and teacher Annette Aguilar-

Ramos, then actress Julia Mueller, although, in each case, the word 'then' could be replaced with 'concurrently'. Somewhere in there he fitted in a fling with radio personality Eleanor Mondale, daughter of former Vice President Walter Mondale. And this doesn't take into account the groupies when touring, including the unfortunate that fell pregnant.

As he told Mueller: 'For me, having sex is like having to take a shit. It has nothing to do with love. It is not a reflection on the woman I am in love with'. Ol' Silver Tongue strikes again! 'They (Dad's girlfriends) never lasted', said Ariel Zevon, which, with chat up lines like that, should come as a surprise to no one on any hemisphere. But it did give him material for his next album. Half the songs on *Mr. Bad Example* were inspired by his complex love life.

Zevon's two albums for Virgin America, *Sentimental Hygiene* and *Transverse City*, saw the singer-songwriter experimenting with new approaches. In the former, he abandoned his usual California crew to hang out with a younger set in the shape of R.E.M.. The result saw Zevon contemporised for the indie era, his songs as carefully crafted as ever, but perhaps lacking their usual West Coast polish, and that was no bad thing. For *Transverse City,* he resurrected that hoary staple of the late 1960s/early 1970s, the concept album, and breathed late 1980s life into it with his fly-eyed vision of imperial, societal and environmental disintegration. They were artistic triumphs in the eyes of many commentators but commercial failures, so one could sympathise with Zevon when he retreated to more-familiar territory for his first solo release on Giant Records.

For *Mr. Bad Example*, Zevon reunited with Wachtel, Lindley, Calderón and others from his heyday gang, right down to photographer Jimmy Wachtel, who took the picture of the cigarette-smoking and sunglasses-sporting skull that Warren dubbed 'Old Velvet Nose'. This mascot would henceforth grace the back covers of every album released in Zevon's lifetime.

In terms of the music, *Mr. Bad Example* may contain a couple of ho-hum moments like 'Things To Do In Denver When You're Dead' and the title track, but despite this, it's an excellent album, with songs like 'Suzie Lightning', 'Renegade', 'Heartache Spoken Here' and 'Searching For A Heart' ranking amongst the finest in the Zevon catalogue.

Incredibly, it tanked, notching up a mere 100,000 units sold, his lowest ever sales, *Wanted Dead Or Alive* aside. Although still contracted for two more albums, the failure of *Mr. Bad Example* and the tainted *hindu love gods* project meant his position as a recording artist for Giant was already in jeopardy.

'Finishing Touches' (Zevon)
Before deciding on a title, Zevon referred to this as 'the hate song', distilling four minutes of vitriol into a hard rock riff. It starts with 'I'm getting tired of you' and builds to 'You can screw everybody I've ever known/But I still won't talk to you on the phone', along the way throwing in the weary, withering dismissal, 'I'm sick and tired, and my cock is sore'.

The core band on *Mr. Bad Example* consisted of Waddy Wachtel on guitar, Bob Glaub on bass and Jeff Porcaro on drums, with Zevon on keyboards and occasional guitar. It's only these four that play on 'Finishing Touches', but the lack of ornamentation works in the song's favour, benefitting from an especially fat riff courtesy of Wachtel. As openers go, it's strong, simple and arresting.

'Suzie Lightning' (Zevon)

A postcard from bassist Bob Glaub in Budapest. Ray 'Boom Boom' Mancini filming *The Dirty Dozen: The Fatal Mission* in Zagreb, then part of Yugoslavia. And, according to the liner notes of the *I'll Sleep When I'm Dead* anthology, 'a composite of women who had recently made me unhappy (and vice versa)'. These are the diverse components that led to one of Zevon's most gorgeous songs, the weightless and gloriously-transcendent 'Suzie Lightning'.

Ethereal and enchanting, the song is built around a series of arpeggiated keyboard descents, around which Wachtel's keening guitar flits and hovers like a hummingbird. This splendid arabesque is all quite intoxicating, but Glaub and Porcaro keep the song grounded with a deceptively simple rhythm. It's a masterclass from all players on their respective instruments, and any current or future Zevon 'best of' that fails to include this track can consider itself incomplete.

A song about a relationship in decay, it is thematically similar to 'Finishing Touches', but the tone is one of resignation rather than rage. Interestingly, it is the only song in the Zevon canon that's completely rhyme-free, but the lyric's vivid snapshots more than compensate for the absence of rhyme.

One other component not mentioned in the opening paragraph is the title. Zevon stole the name from the credits of the 1975 Joan Collins/Donald Pleasance horror movie *I Don't Want To Be Born* (US title *Sharon's Baby*), which listed one Suzie Lightning as a stripper. This is Ms. Lightning's solitary entry in the Internet Movie Database (IMDB).

'Model Citizen' (Waddy Wachtel, LeRoy P. Marinell, Zevon)

The team behind 'Werewolves Of London' reunite for two songs on this album, kicking off with 'Model Citizen'. Less humorous than its hairy predecessor, this song is satirical, its target being self-proclaimed pillars of the community who see themselves as model citizens, but whose thoughts, words and actions suggest they're not as upstanding as they like to think they are. Here, our narrator exhibits irritating traits such as leaving the milk on the porch and never mowing the lawn, which escalates to tormenting the mailman and terrorising the maid, not to mention the narrator's children, before fully revealing his deranged personality by loading up his car and driving it into the lake. Not to worry, though, because as he then informs us, 'I'm a law-abiding man/I'm a good samaritan/I pay my taxes when I can/Model citizen'.

L.A. session guitarist Dan Dugmore joins the core four, as does Jordan Zevon on harmony vocals, the latter making more impact as he and Wachtel sing the song title behind the main character's list of misdemeanours. Despite the presence of Dugmore and Wachtel, it's Zevon who plays the middle and closing guitar solos while also supplying some light, Roy Bittan-like piano figures. 'Model Citizen' might not automatically qualify for a position on Zevon anthologies, but it is a good, solid song.

'Angel Dressed In Black' (Julia Mueller, Wachtel, Zevon)

The quality is maintained with track four, written for and about former *Rolling Stone* journalist – and former Zevon flame – Merle Ginsberg. The song was started after their relationship went belly-up two years earlier, and fittingly, the titular angel is notable for her absence throughout the song, a hole in the narrator's life while he's left 'Sitting on the sofa/Suckin' a bowl of crack'. Curiously, one of the co-writers was current flame Mueller, who herself inevitably became the subject of several Zevon songs.

The guitar and keyboard play the principal chords, which, in a nice bit of studio wizardry, are then treated with echo, and warped, so the music sounds as if it's winding down mid-chord. Wachtel buttresses this with delicate little percussive guitar ostinatos throughout, and the whole piece builds to a rousing Phil Spector-ish wall of sound for the chorus. Despite this nod to the past, it's the closest Zevon ever got to the then-current grunge sound.

A mid-tempo rocker, 'Angel Dressed In Black' is delightfully infectious, and a couple of spins may well find the listener reciting such cheerful couplets as 'She might have been arrested/She might have been attacked/She might be lying dead somewhere/My angel dressed in black'.

'Mr. Bad Example' (Jorge Calderón, Zevon)

Adopting the role of the song's title character, Zevon gleefully admits one outrage after another, beginning as an altar boy burgling his church's charity boxes, and concluding as a corrupt industrialist who increases his profits through suppressing workers' pay and rights. The lyrics were co-written by Zevon and Jorge Calderón, with each wordsmith trying to outdo the other in terms of absurd villainy, resulting in this verbose seven-verse two-chorus breathlessly-delivered song with no instrumental break.

Despite some convincingly brassy keyboards and double drumming from Porcaro and Jim Keltner, those preposterous lyrics combined with the decision to do 'Mr. Bad Example' as a polka means that this is never going to be seen as anything other than a novelty song, and not a particularly funny one at that. Anyone wondering what a Randy Newman/Weird Al Yankovic team-up would sound like need look no further.

The song's only redeeming feature is that it gives *Mr. Bad Example* its killer title.

'Renegade' (Zevon)

From the ridiculous to the sublime. A Chicagoan by way of California is probably not the best qualified to yearn for some romanticised lost south, but

Zevon is role-playing here, singing from the point of view of an embittered former Confederate soldier, setting the song in the Reconstruction era of American history immediately following the Civil War. Much of the old south's values are today best read as a warning from history, but Zevon inhabits his character to sing with surprising sincerity and beauty.

There are some verbal shortcuts that border on cliché (The high school band playing 'Dixieland', and the dream that the south will rise again), but these are offset by well-crafted emotional set-pieces. Thus, our old soldier expresses resigned pragmatism ('We were hopelessly outnumbered/It was a lost cause all along'), feels continuing disappointment ('We ain't seen no reconstruction here/Just the scorched earth all around'), and experiences profound regret ('Next time I would rather break than bend'). *That* south may not be ours or even Zevon's, but it is the south of his unnamed protagonist, who struggles with the collapse of his cultural identity, and this is what Zevon captures so well with his storytelling.

Musically, 'Renegade' is a multifaceted gem. Zevon's voice is probably at its most soulful since 'Mohammed's Radio', and the harmonies by Wachtel, Calderón, Warren and Jordan Zevon are heavenly. Glaub's slow-pulsing bass anchors the track, and Porcaro's subtle drumming morphs nicely into a military cadence by verse two. Wachtel's guitar-playing is warm and lovely, and Zevon adorns the piece with graceful piano and suitably-melancholy keyboards. David Lindley's fiddle is not only in sympathy with the track's mood but enhances its authenticity.

Bafflingly, 'Renegade' is another classic that's never appeared on any Zevon anthology but is a treasure ripe for rediscovery.

'Heartache Spoken Here' (Zevon)

Zevon stays in the south, specifically Nashville, for this, his purest country song since 'Bed Of Coals' on *Bad Luck Streak In Dancing School*. And yep, it's another song that never troubled a 'best of', but really should've.

Lyrically it's another 'poor me' number, Zevon informing us from the get-go that he is 'no stranger to disillusionment', and that he knows 'a thing or two about heartbreak and tears'. The lyric breaks no new ground, but, as with 'Renegade', the sincerity with which Zevon imbues it elevates it into something special. When he sings 'I know it hurts so/When the one you love don't need you', you absolutely believe that he does.

Of course, it doesn't hurt that these words are supported by a rollicking good tune, at once the distillation of a thousand country songs, but also sounding totally fresh. Glaub and Porcaro play like veterans of the Grand Ole Opry, Dan Dugmore returns to lay down some pedal steel, and Wachtel plays some seriously twangy low notes in the solo.

Giant Records' budget was clearly not on par with that of Asylum or Virgin America, so Zevon was afforded only one big-name guest star, in the shape of Dwight Yoakam, who provides sterling vocal support to Zevon's pathos, transforming 'Heartache Spoken Here' from a fine country song into a durn fine country song.

'Quite Ugly One Morning' (Zevon)

Waddy Wachtel unleashes his inner Tony Iommi on the riff for 'Quite Ugly One Morning', while David Lindley deploys a saz and a cümbü , giving an unexpected Turkish flavour. It's an odd juxtaposition of east-meets-west – Birmingham, England meets Asian Istanbul – but as nifty little fusions go, it works surprisingly well. Later, Zevon indulges in some wordless vocal calls, reminiscent of Scottish punky art-poppers The Skids, and Wachtel and Lindley's combined efforts suddenly evoke the work of the late Stuart Adamson. This is presumably coincidence, as Dunfermline's finest never bothered the US charts, so the likelihood of them registering with Zevon and company is low.

A play on the Dylan Thomas memoir *Quite Early One Morning*, 'Quite Ugly One Morning' in turn loaned its title to a novel by Scottish crime writer Christopher Brookmyre.

'Things To Do In Denver When You're Dead' (Marinell, Wachtel, Zevon)

The 'Werewolves' team get together for the final time and go out with a whimper. Lyrically, it's transparent that the title came first and was then lumbered with a set of jokey, not very interesting, self-referential lyrics: 'I called up my friend LeRoy on the phone/I said, "Buddy, I'm afraid to be alone'. Alas, 'my friend LeRoy' soon found himself *persona non grata* on Planet Zevon, having had the temerity to (rightly) question his 'Werewolves' royalties.

Musically, it's memorable for the wrong reason, featuring as it does the single worst keyboard sound of Warren's career, a tinny and toy-like sound reminiscent of the earliest handheld Casios.

This song became the album's second track to bequeath its title, this time to a forgettable Tarantino-lite 1995 movie starring Andy Garcia, Christopher Walken and Christopher Lloyd.

'Searching For A Heart' (Zevon)

The quality control gets cranked back to the max for the album closer. This was written in reaction to Zevon's breakup with Annette Aguilar-Ramos, who is presumably one of the 'certain individuals' in the opening verse who 'aren't sticking with the plan'. There's desperation ('I'm searching for a heart/Searching everyone') and hope ('They say love conquers all/You can't start it like a car/You can't stop it with a gun'), and finally, in song if not in life, reconciliation ('Certain individuals have finally come around').

Musically, everyone is at the top of their game. Zevon had been blessed over the years with a terrific array of world-class rhythm sections, but, based on their contributions to *Mr. Bad Example*, Bob Glaub and Jeff Porcaro might just be the best, with their work on 'Searching for a Heart' the jewel in their crown. Sadly, this was to be Porcaro's last outing with Zevon, as he died from a heart attack the following year, aged 38. The rhythm section here grounds Zevon's organic, breathy keyboard washes and Wachtel's chiming Byrdsian guitar. Adding to the arrangement's gorgeousness are the lush, heavenly harmonies of Calderón, and Michael, Mark and Kipp Lennon of the band Venice.

'Searching For A Heart' positively shimmers, and like 'Splendid Isolation', it's a hit that should've been. Even its prominent placement in the movies *Love At Large* (1990) and *Grand Canyon* (1991) failed to help the single dent the chart.

Related songs
'Casey Jones' (Jerry Garcia, Robert Hunter)
Credited to Warren Zevon with David Lindley, this was recorded for the 1991 album *Deadicated: A Tribute to the Grateful Dead*. It's a slightly more rocky but ultimately too-faithful copy of the bluesy folk original, its main point of interest being the presence of Ian McLagan of the Small Faces and Faces on Hammond B-3 organ.

Mutineer (1995)

Personnel:
Warren Zevon: vocals, piano, keyboards, guitar, percussion
Peter Asher: harmony vocals on 'The Indifference Of Heaven'
Rosemary Butler: harmony vocals on 'Jesus Was A Cross Maker' and 'Mutineer'
Jorge Calderón: bass on 'Seminole Bingo'; harmony vocals on 'Poisonous Lookalike'
Bruce Hornsby: accordion on 'Piano Fighter' and 'Monkey Wash Donkey Rinse'
Larry Klein: bass on 'Rottweiler Blues' and 'Mutineer'
David Lindley: fiddle and cittern on 'Poisonous Lookalike'; fiddle on 'Monkey Wash Donkey Rinse'
Michael Wolff: keyboards on 'Similar To Rain'
Producer: Warren Zevon
Recorded at Devonshire Studios, North Hollywood, CA
Release date: 23 May 1995
Label: Giant
Chart placing: Did not chart
Running time: 35:37

Zevon toured *Mr. Bad Example* with Canadian power poppers Odds as his backing band, but following the album's poor showing at the cash desk, Giant slashed Zevon's recording and touring budget. From now on, he would largely be a one-man band in concert, a self-proclaimed 'heavy metal folk singer'.

He had been there before, in the mid-1980s when between record deals, so it was a style of performing he'd perfected. So Zevon proposed that his next album be a live document of his solo shows, reasoning that it would cost considerably less than a new studio outing and that it would allow him to put out a 'best of' that capitalised on the *MTV Unplugged* concert and album series. Giant agreed, and the result was 1993's live *Learning to Flinch* album, which will be discussed later.

Amidst all this enforced downsizing, a new opportunity opened up in film and television music. His songs had enjoyed some intermittent big-screen outings since 'He Quit Me' formed part of the *Midnight Cowboy* soundtrack in 1969; a live Linda Ronstadt take of 'Poor Poor Pitiful Me' appears in *FM* (1978) while her studio version plays during *The Entity* (1982); 'Werewolves Of London' appears in a 1981 episode of the television series *Chorus,* and more famously in the scene where Tom Cruise dances around the pool table in *The Color of Money* (1986); 'Leave My Monkey Alone' crops up in the TV movie *Tarzan in Manhattan* (1989); 'Johnny Strikes Up the Band' is in *Heaven Tonight* (1990); and, as mentioned earlier, 'Searching For A Heart' appears in both *Love at Large* and *Grand Canyon*, the latter also featuring 'Lawyers, Guns, and Money'.

All this provided Zevon with additional exposure and some extra ker-ching in his coffers, but in the early 1990s he began receiving invitations to produce music for television shows. He provided incidental music for Michael Mann's three-part 1990 TV series *Drug Wars: The Camarena Story*, scored the 1992 *Tales of the Crypt* episode 'King Of The Road', supplied songs in the style of famous artists and wrote incidental music for *Route 66* (1993), and provided the theme and additional music for William Shatner's TV series *Tekwars* the following year. These songs will be discussed in a later chapter.

Meanwhile, work on his fourth album for Giant continued. Keeping costs to a minimum, he recorded much of it at his yet-to-be-christened home studio Anatomy of a Headache, playing most of the instruments himself. He enjoyed the autonomy this granted him, later telling *Mojo*'s Andy Gill: 'Making *Mutineer* was very enjoyable, which is not something I could say about the recording process over the years in general'. He even took the front sleeve shot himself, perhaps making *Mutineer* the first album with a selfie on the cover.

Mutineer has a clutch of excellent songs in 'Poisonous Lookalike', 'The Indifference Of Heaven' and 'Something Bad Happened To A Clown'. But good though they are, they fall short of the high bar set by the likes of 'Desperados Under the Eaves', 'Roland The Headless Thompson Gunner' and 'Splendid Isolation'. At the other end of the scale there is 'Similar To Rain', with the distinctly so-so 'Rottweiler Blues' hovering slightly above this, while everything else can be mapped at different points in the middle to upper half of the range. In other words, it's not the album anyone should buy or be given as their introduction to Zevon, that honour being reserved for his Asylum catalogue, *Sentimental Hygiene*, or a couple of his later works.

Entertainment Weekly's Dimitri Ehrlich gave the album a B+, stating, 'Despite occasional obtuse melodies and a few obnoxious guitar solos, *Mutineer* is worth careful scrutiny'. It praises Zevon as 'an intelligence rare in pop', calling the title track 'a ballad as sad and honest as they come'. Writing for *Louisville Music News*, Bob Bahr summarised the album as 'an uneven, adventurous record'. Both this statement and the B+ rating were indicative of critical response across the board.

To quote 'The Indifference Of Heaven', it was 'the same old story, the same old tune'. The critics liked it, but it was a commercial flop, failing to find a new audience, while playing to a decreasing number of existing fans. Zevon's four-record deal with Giant had come to a close, and his contract was not renewed. As was the case when Asylum dropped him, it would be another five years before he resurfaced.

'Seminole Bingo' (Carl Hiaasen, Zevon)
'Seminole Bingo' is flash fiction in song. A white-collar criminal on the run ends up at Florida's Big Cypress Reservation, where he becomes addicted to the bingo games run by members of the Seminole Tribe. He soon finds his ill-gotten gains depleting rapidly, as 'All my Wall Street wiles don't help me even slightly/'Cause I never have the numbers, and I'm losing nightly'.

This comic crime caper was co-written by American novelist Carl Hiaasen, of whom Zevon, an avid crime fiction buff, was a long-standing fan. The songwriter was delighted to discover that it was a two-way street, Hiaasen having made one of the main characters in his 1991 novel *Native Tongue* a huge Zevon fan. The pair subsequently met at a book signing, and a firm friendship was formed. The phrase 'Seminole bingo' comes from a tourist brochure Zevon picked up in Florida while visiting Hiaasen, and the album title comes from a Floridian tourist stop Zevon caught sight of on the same trip.

Though Hiaasen supplied much of the lyric, the music was all down to Zevon, except for the bass played by Jorge Calderón. Unfortunately, Zevon's muddy drumming swamps Calderón's efforts. The singer fares better on guitar, pulling off a convincing Waddy Wachtel impersonation, and he balances some raunchy little solos with featherlight piano figures.

Verse one is of special note:

I'm a junk bond king
And I'm on the run
Me and a friend of mine
We were heading for the sunshine

When singing it, Zevon perfectly stresses both syllables of the final word 'sunshine', so the first syllable rhymes with the 'run' at the end of line two, and the second rhymes with the 'mine' at the end of line three. Slight it may seem, but it's a lovely poetical flourish, deftly done.

'Something Bad Happened To A Clown' (Zevon)

In *The Brady Bunch Movie* (1995), aspiring folk singer Greg Brady tries to woo a girl with his composition 'Clowns Never Laughed Before', only to be cruelly slapped down with the words, 'No one writes songs about clowns anymore'. Well, here's the mutinous Mr. Zevon, the very year that movie was released, doing precisely that, and thank goodness he is, for what a wonderfully warped little gem it is.

There's that captivating and evocative title for starters, a phrase that instantly validates Jackson Browne's description of Zevon as 'the first and foremost proponent of song noir'. And like any good mystery, the listener is drawn in, intrigued to find out what *exactly* happened to the white-faced buffoon. This is never made clear because Warren opts for the less-is-more approach, leaving it to his audience to fill in the blanks. All we know is that 'Someone lost their squirting rose/There's his red nose on the ground', 'She doesn't think he's very funny anymore', and, ominously, there are 'Footsteps in the sawdust leading to the edge of town'.

Zevon creates a Wurlitzer organ sound to give the song an appropriate circus feel, but, in keeping with the song title, the playing is somewhat discordant and off-kilter, 'like the sound of a running down calliope', to quote an earlier song. A variety of percussive instruments enhances the track's overall three-ring fever dream quality, and a couple of squealing guitar solos cap things off.

'Similar To Rain' (Zevon)

Oh dear. This album was going so well, and then along came 'Similar To Rain'. The discordancy of the previous song remains, but it's without the knowing playfulness, and all melody has been rooted out, leaving this sounding like something The Asylum film company would come up with if they produced Disney-style tunes instead of mockbusters.

'The Indifference Of Heaven' (Zevon)

According to Zevon, this was 'the first of many depressing songs about the departure of my flaxen-tressed fiancée' (Julia Mueller), and the lyric style was inspired by the works of British author Martin Amis, in general, and by his 1991 novel *Time's Arrow* in particular. The song, complete with yet another great noir title, was first aired on the live *Learning to Flinch* record but makes its studio debut here. Like the live take, it's a twelve-string-driven thing, but some military-style marching drums make it statelier than its predecessor, while Peter Asher's harmonious embellishments lend one of Zevon's heaviest, most downcast numbers the slightest glimmer of light.

A brace of Springsteen-esque buzzwords suggests he was as much an influence as Amis, while American author Flannery O'Connor's Southern Gothic energy positively fizzes in lines like 'Time on my hands/Time to kill/ Blood on my hands/And my hands in the till'. Meanwhile, *Something Else*'s Kasper Nijsen rightly hailed the brilliant 'I had a girl/Now she's gone/She left town/Town burned down/Nothing left but the sound/Of the front door closing forever' as 'a miracle of concise and dramatic songwriting'.

'Jesus Was a Cross Maker' (Judee Sill)

This song was originally the first single by fellow Asylum alumni Judee Sill, although she and Zevon were not on the label concurrently. It was released in 1971, and, like all her work issued in her lifetime, was met with indifference, although a cover version by the Hollies enjoyed some chart success in New Zealand two years later.

Zevon slows the song to a glacial pace, which increases its gospel flavour, a feeling reinforced by Rosemary Butler's benedictory backing vocals. Zevon's instrument of choice is a droning harmonium, presumably selected to enhance the song's gospel feel, but this, along with the synth strings and sampled celesta, somewhat negates Butler's uplifting presence, and transforms Sill's best-known number into a tired dirge. He also cuts it in half, ditching the third verse and the repeated first. He may get kudos for doing it his way, but his way will send most listeners scurrying for the original.

'Poisonous Lookalike' (Zevon)

Another noir-ish title, this time a botanical term describing toxic plants that bear a startling resemblance to edible ones. Zevon heard the phrase on a radio show, and uses it to describe how someone in a long-term relationship can change so much that their partner no longer recognises them. In other words, they become a poisonous lookalike of the person he first met.

'Poisonous Lookalike' isn't as magisterial as 'The Indifference Of Heaven' or as ornate as 'Something Bad Happened To A Clown', but it is a lot more fun and is probably *Mutineer*'s standout track. It has a ramshackle indie vibe that was right at home in the mid-1990s, though it's also reminiscent of pre-arena R.E.M.. David Lindley plays a cittern to great effect, lending the song a surprising jauntiness that is contrapuntal to Warren's weary tone.

Jorge Calderón also adds important textural balance. The list of Zevon's past vocalists reads like a who's-who of L.A.'s shiniest – from Linda Ronstadt to Lindsey Buckingham, Stevie Nicks and assorted Eagles – but, from the unsung Calderón's shouted Spanish in 'I'll Sleep When I'm Dead' to being part of the heavenly harmonies on 'Searching For A Heart', he has consistently delivered the goods, and again comes up trumps here. He doesn't just echo Zevon, but instead sends his voice soaring whenever Warren's descends, adding a sweetness that balances Zevon's bitter delivery.

This is not to suggest that Lindley or Calderón carry Zevon. He is in top form, be it with his spectral guitar flourishes, a scything solo, keyboards that sound like the soundtrack to a funfair ghost train, simple repetitive percussive patterns that keep the song grounded, or the pleasing elongated guitar note that serves as the conclusion.

Released as the album's second single, the track's strings-centric approach could have ushered it into charts that, thanks to the US grunge movement and the UK Britpop scene, had fallen in love with guitar music again. Sadly, *Mutineer* was Zevon's most invisible record, and 'Poisonous Lookalike' collapsed into the same black hole.

'Piano Fighter' (Zevon)

This is the second *Mutineer* song that was test-driven on *Learning to Flinch*, an album that was originally going to be called *Piano Fighter,* until Zevon realised he had 'to make every effort to resist the temptation to be grandiose'.

The first sound heard is Bruce Hornsby's accordion, which remains prominent throughout, but is particularly so on the opening verse and chorus, where it conveys a woozy bar room atmosphere. Meanwhile, Zevon plays like a beginner tinkling on a toy piano, tying in with the autobiographical lyrics, 'Mom and Papa bought a Chickering/Every day I'd sit and play that thing/I practiced hard'.

In verse two, the toy keyboard effect is replaced by a glockenspiel, briefly hogging the spotlight until drums, bass, acoustic and electric guitars join in, all played by Zevon, who also sings his own harmony vocals. It sounds like a banjo is added to the mix by the time we arrive at the second chorus, by which time the lyrics relate to Zevon circa mid-Sixties to early Seventies, when 'I worked in sessions and I played in bands'.

After a middle eight as tipsy as the pink elephant scene in *Dumbo*, the final verse maintains the above instrumentation but with more frenetic drumming and keyboards verging on techno. By this time, the narrator has reached the tail-end of the 1970s, when he 'cut a record and it made the charts'.

With all its cuts and changes, 'Piano Fighter' runs the risk of having musical ants in its pants, but its more intricate arrangement, richer textures and more-rounded mood, renders it superior to the solo piano version on *Learning to Flinch*.

'Rottweiler Blues' (Hiaasen, Zevon)

Carl Hiaasen returns for 'Rottweiler Blues' and considering the titles of all his adult fiction books consist of just two words, it highly possibly he coined this one too.

It's a hard rock number like 'Seminole Bingo', but it is strictly so-so, being less successful musically and lyrically. Whereas the album opener had a story to tell, this song sketches a survivalist nutjob that has a Glock handgun in his bedside table, a machine gun by the bedroom door, and a Kevlar vest he wears to go shopping. His biggest defence mechanism, however, is his Rottweiler, 'One hundred pounds of unfriendly persuasion/Sleeping on the Florida porch'. Visitors are advised against calling, 'If you don't know my Rottweiler's name'.

Session player and producer Larry Klein is on bass, but one must wonder why Zevon called in such an established player, only to partner him with drumming so rudimentary it borders on the primitive.

'Monkey Wash Donkey Rinse' (Duncan Aldrich, Zevon)

According to Zevon, this bizarre title refers to a monkey he saw in Marrakesh that had been 'trained to jerk off a donkey'. Meanwhile, co-writer Duncan Aldrich lays claim to coining the phrase, which he explains was his 'impression of an R.E.M. all-access pass', which, as explanations go, is every bit as obscure as the original phrase. Neither account has any obvious connection to the lyric.

It's a lively little tune, sounding very much like some traditional American folk song, and it's easy to imagine it being performed at early 19th-century social gatherings in such rural upstate New York locations as Tarrytown or Sleepy Hollow. David Lindley on fiddle and Bruce Hornsby on accordion serve to reinforce this notion. The lyric *is* about a social gathering, specifically 'A party in the centre of the earth', where 'Hell is only half full'. According to ol' Mr. Glass-half-empty, it is where we will all be bound, come the 'twilight of the gods'.

'Mutineer' (Zevon)

All the songs on what would traditionally have been side two have mid-to-fast tempos, so Zevon opts to down gears and conclude with a dreamy slice of lo-fi sunshine pop. In keeping with the nautical song title, it comprises rolling keyboard washes that shimmer like the late evening sun reflected on still summer waters. The song's weightlessness is anchored by a returning Larry Klein, who here is given room to flex, weaving his bass lines around Zevon's synths, and he neatly offsets Warren's minimalist percussion with his understated complexity.

Writing in the sleeve notes of the *I'll Sleep When I'm Dead* anthology, Zevon called 'Mutineer' a 'gesture of appreciation and affection to my fans, none of whom bought the record'. It's hard to tell whether that last part was delivered bitterly or with wry humour, but Bob Dylan certainly enjoyed 'Mutineer' enough to perform it in concert as a tribute to Zevon after his terminal illness was announced, a recording of which was later included in the *Enjoy Every Sandwich* tribute album.

Related songs
'Jackhammer' (Steven Drake, Doug Elliott, Craig Northey, Paul Brennan)
You would think that with all the guests on Zevon's records over the years he would be asked to reciprocate every so often, but apparently no one ever did. But he was invited to contribute to this track recorded by Odds, who had served as his backing band on the *Mr. Bad Example* tour. It appeared on their 1993 album *Bedbugs*. Zevon doesn't particularly stand out – he trades guitar licks with Robert Quine (Richard Hell, Lou Reed, etc.) – but, discounting his work for hire for the Everly Brothers in the early 1970s, this marks his first time as a guest on someone else's record since his reputed appearance on Phil Ochs' *Pleasures of the Harbour* in 1967.

'Running Through/Chinese Poem Sing' (Jack Kerouac)
Zevon recorded this Jack Kerouac piece for the 1997 Rykodisc spoken-word tribute album *Kerouac: Kicks Joy Darkness*. Zevon's delivery is flawless, as would be expected of one so well versed in poetry, although there is a tendency to overextend the oft-repeated word 'wine'. Musical accompaniment comes from jazz pianist Michael Wolff, who played on the *Mutineer* track 'Similar To Rain'.

Life'll Kill Ya (2000)

Personnel:
Warren Zevon: vocals, guitar, keyboards, piccolo, pennywhistle, theremin,
percussion
Jorge Calderón: vocals, bass, percussion
Winston Watson: drums, percussion
Chuck Prophet: guitar on 'For My Next Trick I'll Need A Volunteer'
Jimmy Ryan: mandolin on 'Ourselves To Know'
Babi Floyd, Dennis Collins, Curtis King: vocals on 'Fistful Of Rain'
Producers: Paul Q. Kolderie, Sean Slade
Recorded at Anatomy of a Headache, Los Angeles; Fort Apache, Cambridge,
Massachusetts; The Magic Shop, New York
Release date: 25 January 2000
Label: Artemis
Chart Placing: US: 173
Running time: 40:23

Zevon was back to playing solo shows to keep the roof over his head, but had income from other sources too. In 1996, Rhino Records released the career-spanning two-CD set *I'll Sleep When I'm Dead* (although *Wanted Dead or Alive* continued to be ignored). A smart looking box set, it might've tempted the curious, but the inclusion of four previously-unreleased tracks surely also ensnared the faithful (These will be reviewed later).

The following year, Zevon was asked to fill in for bandleader Paul Shaffer for a fortnight on *The Late Show with David Letterman*, which led to further substitute gigs. 1997 also saw Zevon play some shows at the Miami Book Fair with the Rock Bottom Remainders, a fundraising band comprising published authors and writers such as Stephen King, Amy Tan, Dave Barry, Mitch Alborn, and others. In the words of member Dave Barry, they 'play music as well as Metallica writes novels'. Although it was not a money-spinner, Zevon, a voracious reader, would have been thrilled to be in such literary company, while, for their part, the writers admitted to being in awe of the rock star in their midst.

Zevon branched into acting, appearing as himself in HBO's *Dream On*, *The Larry Sanders Show*, and two episodes of *Suddenly Susan*, an NBC sitcom starring Brooke Shields. He also starred as Mr. Babcock, the mute sidekick of Billy Bob Thornton's *Brigadier General Smalls*, in Dwight Yoakam's universally deplored western *South of Heaven, West of Hell*. The same year, Zevon was asked to provide the theme music for the Fox TV show *Action*, a dark comedy scathing in its account of Hollywood culture. The deal ultimately fell through, although the show used the ready-made and equally scathing 'Even A Dog Can Shake Hands', from *Sentimental Hygiene*.

Through all this, Warren continued working on new songs, uncertain as to where or when they would see the light of day. Meanwhile, behind the scenes, a familiar guardian angel was at work. Just as he had pressed David Geffen to offer Zevon a record contract a quarter of a century earlier, Jackson Browne now approached Danny Goldberg – who was launching a new record label – and suggested he should sign Zevon. Browne assured Goldberg that Zevon's new material was as good as anything he'd ever written. Upon hearing the songs, Goldberg agreed, and Warren had a new home at Artemis Records.

Zevon released two very strong albums after long studio absences, *Warren Zevon* (1976) and *Sentimental Hygiene* (1987), and *Life'll Kill Ya* completes that hat trick of top-form comeback albums. Sure, there are weak spots like 'Hostage-O' and 'My Shit's Fucked Up', and that thoroughly inoffensive Steve Winwood cover will forever hover between take it or leave it, but the strength of the remaining songs makes this album a glittering jewel in the Zevon crown.

Like *Mutineer*, much of *Life'll Kill Ya* was recorded at Warren's home studio Anatomy of a Headache, though the album is not as spartan as its predecessor, and has a much warmer timbre. It's further bolstered by a gifted rhythm section in Calderón and drummer Winston Watson, lending the album a greater consistency than *Mutineer* had. Adding focus was Zevon's insistence that *Life'll Kill Ya* was a folk record, even knocking back Calderón's offer of drafting in Waddy Wachtel, because he didn't want it to become 'a big rock guitar album'. In the end, it was closer to that folk-rock hybrid, Americana, than undistilled folk, though 'Porcelain Monkey' demonstrates that Zevon couldn't completely shake loose his rock and roll roots.

Critically, the album was well-received. Writing in *The Independent*, Nick Hasted called it 'As fitting a comeback for a 50-something rock'n'roller as Dylan's *Time Out of Mind*', and it appeared in many a publication's year-end 'best of' lists. Commercially, some chart statistics suggested it might be time to pop the cork on that two-litre bottle of Mountain Dew to celebrate. *Life'll Kill Ya* was Warren's first album in the downloadable music age, and it reached 9 in the internet albums chart, and managed one spot higher in the US independent chart. However, where it mattered, the figures were more sobering. It put Warren back in the *Billboard* 200 for the first time since *Sentimental Hygiene*, but a whopping 110 places south of that album's number 63. It may only have reached a lowly 146 in the UK, but, staggeringly, it was his first album to enter the British charts.

The sales figures must've been a devastating blow for Zevon and Artemis. Despite all the positive reviews and the supporting tour with all its affiliated press, radio and television appearances, it was that well-furrowed same old story, same old tune once more. *Life'll Kill Ya* sold 30,000 copies.

'I Was In The House When The House Burned Down' (Zevon)

Presumably cognizant of the weakness of his own performances on *Mutineer*, Zevon enlisted longtime collaborator Calderón and new recruit Winston Watson on bass and drums, respectively. As a huge Dylan fan, Zevon would've been aware of the drummer from his four-year stint on Dylan's Never Ending

Tour (1992-1996), and from Dylan's *MTV Unplugged* album. A versatile player, Watson was also behind the kit for Alice Cooper's 1998 School's Out for Summer tour.

Calderón and Watson make an immediate impact on the opening track, a terrific Dylanesque song every bit as strong as 'Sentimental Hygiene', the last song to signal the end of a five-year hiatus. Driven by acoustic guitar and harmonica, 'I Was In The House' is a far more folky beast than its rocky predecessor, and Zevon's playing is both vibrant and dramatic. It's as if the presence of a superior rhythm section, especially Watson's sublime and sloppy tub-thumping, has challenged the singer to up his game.

The lyric is equally as strong, that arresting title matched by the opening line, 'I had the shit till it all got smoked'. When this track was chosen to be the album's lead single, the word 'shit' had to be changed into something more radio-friendly. Zevon hummed and hawed, wondering if to do so was to squander his artistic integrity. It was only when Goldberg pointed out that writer Allen Ginsberg had frequently toned down his material for broadcasting purposes that the singer acquiesced.

'I Was in the House' saw Warren hitting unusually high and potentially painful notes on each verse's penultimate line, something he'd obviously practised in the studio but never attempted to replicate live

'Life'll Kill Ya' (Zevon)

This is surely popular music's most jaunty and delightful song about death. It's a treat both musically and lyrically. 'Tell Laura I Love Her' it ain't.

The lyric starts with the bizarre but undoubtedly cruel insult, 'You've got an invalid haircut'. Although the song is about death and dying, the first verse doesn't go there, instead offering up a series of playfully-surreal lines that serve as a masterclass in scansion. Take the following four lines:

> It's the kingdom of the spiders
> It's the empire of the ants
> You need a license to walk around downtown
> You need a permit to dance

Why Zevon feels the need to reference a pair of ropey 'nature strikes back' sci-fi horror flicks from 1977 is something of a mystery. Perhaps he was giving a nod to old *TekWar* boss William Shatner who starred in *Kingdom of the Spiders*, or perhaps it simply scans well, and 'ants' kind of rhymes with 'dance'. Despite being penned by someone often tarred with the intellectual brush, this neatly reinforces Zevon's fondness for lowbrow entertainment, a fact further illustrated in his diary entry for 16 January 1997, where he delights in taking Ariel to see *Scream*, calling himself her 'junk culture emissary'.

The chorus gleefully states the obvious, 'Life'll kill ya/Then you'll be dead', before leading into a second verse that all but celebrates death's inevitability.

93

The opening four lines are worth noting:

From the President of the United States
To the lowliest rock and roll star
The doctor is in and he'll see you now
He don't care who you are

The lowly rock star is, of course, Warren, but the doctor he describes isn't some helpful healer but the grim reaper himself. Zevon admitted to a phobia regarding doctors, believing that if you went to see one, you'd only receive bad news. In his eyes, medical practitioners were there not to make you better, but to confirm the worst-case scenario. This was borne out two years later when Zevon was diagnosed with one of 'the awful, awful diseases' mentioned later in this verse.

'Life'll Kill Ya' is piano-led, Zevon introducing the song with a sprightly, one-handed flourish before bass, drums and acoustic guitar join in when the vocals begin. At the tail end of the track, the process is reversed, Calderón and Watson bowing out once the words are done, leaving Zevon to reprise his mono-handed tinkling, repeating the opening piano pattern before terminating it abruptly and effectively.

'Porcelain Monkey' (Jorge Calderón, Zevon)
Zevon switches to guitar for this fast rocker in which he and co-writer Calderón capture the last days of Elvis Presley with the precision of novelists. Great lines abound, but these three stand out in particular: 'Left behind by the latest trends/Eating fried chicken with his regicidal friends/That's how the story ends'. The junk food diet, the Memphis Mafia, the sense of insulation and isolation, the incapacity to change with the times; the twilight of the king is expertly summarised in less than 20 words, an astonishing piece of shorthand that presents the listener with a full picture.

The melody matches the lyric in quality, with some robust guitar soloing and gorgeous Hammond organ washes, but it's the rapid upstroke/downstroke combo on the third line of the chorus that proves to be the kicker.

The title derives from an ornament with onyx eyes that Presley had in his TV room in Graceland. The song came about when Zevon spotted a postcard depicting the room stuck to Calderón's fridge. The titular monkey can still be viewed by visitors to Graceland today. 'Porcelain Monkey' is the fifth and final Zevon song with a simian in the title. Can any other act in popular music match or, better, this odd statistic?

'For My Next Trick I'll Need A Volunteer' (Zevon)
That sly black humour makes its presence felt in the opening lines, 'I can saw a woman in two/But you won't want to look in the box when I do'. But this song is less about magic and more about loss. 'I can make love disappear',

sings Zevon despairingly, 'For my next trick, I'll need a volunteer'. It's another end-of-relationship song, but the humour and the novel approach keeps the familiar subject matter fresh.

The piano and harmonica are the dominant instruments, and Zevon plays them and sings in an almost vaudevillian way, creating the aural illusion of something new being comfortable and old-fashioned, a trick that, for example, American author Garrison Keillor was similarly able to pull off with his *A Prairie Home Companion* radio show.

'I'll Slow You Down' (Zevon)

Another song about a failing relationship, this presents a narrator that's tired of perceived abuse. His complaints are both surreal ('You know I hate it when you put your hand inside my head/And switch all my priorities around') and juvenile ('Why don't you pick on someone your own size instead?'), but he resolves to call it a day ('Go on without me/I'll just slow you down').

The song is almost a sonic bookend to 'Poisonous Lookalike' from *Mutineer*, with a lovely lilting guitar replacing that song's rancorous chords. Zevon sings in a higher key than usual, Calderón supplies superior harmonies and supple bass, and Watson sits effectively behind the beat. One thing all the *Life'll Kill Ya* songs have in common is they've all been composed with solo performance in mind, but it is such a shame that Artemis didn't stump up the pennies to send Calderón and Watson out on the supporting tour. There is some multitracking on the album to fill out the sound, but this trio would've sounded great live.

'Hostage-O' (Zevon)

It wouldn't truly be a Zevon album without some wobble in the quality control, and along it comes now. But who woulda thunk an ode to bondage, dominance, and sadomasochism could sound so stupefyingly dull? Being able to achieve this is surely some sort of perverse talent in itself.

Calderón's bass rumbles in the background, but this is largely Warren plus acoustic guitar, although the mid-section does contain a short burst of pennywhistle to startle awake anyone that inevitably nodded off during this snoozer.

'Dirty Little Religion' (Zevon)

Things improve here, though, without quite hitting the starry heights of the opening fistful of tracks. This is a fun number, more countrified than folky. The lyric conflates sex with religion, and it's difficult to tell whether Zevon is warning about the ulterior motives of cult leaders, attacking the hypocrisy of evangelists of the Jim Bakker/Jimmy Swaggart mould, or just serving up a devilish slice of whimsy. Perhaps it involves a bit of all three.

Though uncredited, producers Paul Q. Kolderie and Sean Slade provide gruff backing vocals. They'd previously worked with the Mighty Mighty Bosstones and Uncle Tupelo, and had produced Hole's multi-platinum 1994 album *Live*

Through This, but it was their work on Radiohead's debut album *Pablo Honey* that grabbed Zevon's attention, as he was a big admirer of the English band.

'Back In The High Life Again' (Steve Winwood, Will Jennings)

Cover versions, which Zevon had only dabbled in sporadically in the past, would become a staple of his Artemis recordings, starting with this rendering of Steve Winwood's 1986 hit. With its sparse arrangement and elegiac pace, Warren makes the song his own, singing more with hope than with Winwood's certainty.

'My Shit's Fucked Up' (Zevon)

> Well, I went to the doctor
> I said I'm feeling kind of rough
> He said I'll break it to you, son
> Your shit's fucked up

These opening lines would prove to be prophetic a couple of years after they were written, their initial drollness negated by a newfound irony. Calderón and Watson cleverly conjure up a subtle menace, but their efforts are ill-served by the glib lyric, which is beneath Zevon, who comes across like a kid dared to say a sweary word. Despite its prescience, it's hard to see this song as anything other than a disposable novelty.

The song title was left off the tracklisting on the back of the album sleeve, and earned the man who once sung about a murderous adolescent rapist and a bloody headless spectre his first parental-advisory sticker. He performed it live on the long-running BBC music show *Later... with Jools Holland*, allegedly at the insistence of the show's producer. In an interview with Holland, Zevon quipped that it made him feel like 'the dirty John Denver'.

'Fistful Of Rain' (Calderón, Zevon)

The album's longest track is another that sounds like it could've hailed from a previous century while simultaneously sounding timeless. It is lifted by the harmonies of seasoned backing singers Babi Floyd, Dennis Collins and Curtis King, who give this folky tune a gentle gospel inflection, and the piccolo solo adds a fresh texture. It might not be a classic, but it is an enjoyable, well-crafted, expertly delivered song.

'Ourselves To Know' (Zevon)

Although the content differs, this song shares its title with a 1960 John O'Hara novel, presumably intentional on Zevon's part, as he would've been familiar with O'Hara, one of America's most prolific 20th-century authors. The tune, meanwhile, is reminiscent of *Tunnel of Love*-era Springsteen, particularly the harmonica, though this could be more coincidence than conscious. However, one musical component that's very un-Bossy is the wonderful percussion foundation. It is intricate, almost lyrical in structure, and like nothing else found in the Zevon canon. Sadly, it is impossible to say who is responsible for this as the sleeve credits Zevon, Caldern and Watson with percussion, so it could be any one of them, or a combination of more than one. Either way, it's the song's standout feature. Jimmy Ryan, formerly of alt-country band Blood Oranges, adds further texture on mandolin.

Zevon looks to history for inspiration for the first time since *Mr. Bad Example*'s 'Renegade', setting his opening verse in 1099, the final year of the First Crusade, with the narrator seeking to 'restore the one true cross' to Jerusalem. Verse two, which informs us 'Everyone got famous, everyone got rich/Everyone went off the rails and ended in the ditch', is more open to interpretation. The lyrics could still be continuing the crusaders' story, many of whom were given a hero's welcome upon their return from the Holy Land, granted land, titles and other rewards. The second line could refer to those responsible for Christian atrocities against both Muslim and Jew, and to those that met their end during the Crusade. However, since it lacks the scene-setting elements that punctuate verse one (Constantinople, 1099, Jerusalem, Rhodes), Warren could equally be referring to the L.A. scene of the 1960s/1970s. It seems a stretch, but the line that closes each verse – 'We took that holy ride, ourselves to know' – connects both scenarios, each a journey of self-discovery, whether through holy vows or through music and other stimulants.

The third verse further suggests that each stanza depicts a different scenario, as Zevon now directly addresses the listener, informing them that the best way to find yourself is to be righteous in how you treat others. Zevon advises loyalty to those you know and chivalry to 'strangers you meet along the road', all of which brings the lyric full circle, as crusaders invariably believed themselves to be righteous, loyal and chivalrous.

Fittingly for a lyrically introspective song, 'Ourselves To Know' is a quiet classic.

'Don't Let Us Get Sick' (Zevon)

The album concludes with a quiet prayer that we neither get sick, old or stupid, but rather we be brave, play nice, and be together tonight. It's an unadorned benediction, just Warren and guitar, and it's simply lovely.

Melody-wise, it has a definite Celtic air, and bears a passing resemblance to 'The Banks O' Doon' by Scotland's national bard Robert Burns. This may be no coincidence, as Zevon certainly knew his Scottish poets, once casually quoting medieval versifier William Dunbar in a *Guardian* interview, and performing Burns' 'Such A Parcel Of Rogues In A Nation' to open his encore at the Old Fruitmarket, Glasgow, in May 2000.

My Ride's Here (2002)

Personnel:
Warren Zevon: vocals, guitar, keyboards
Sheldon Gomberg: bass
Anton Fig: drums
Katy Salvidge: pennywhistle, fiddle
Sid McGuiness: guitar on 'Hit Somebody'
Paul Schaffer: organ on 'Hit Somebody'
Tony Levin: bass on 'Hit Somebody'
Michael Wolff: organ on 'You're A Whole Different Person When You're Scared'
Joel Derouin, Charlie Bisharat, Evan Wilson, Larry Corbett: string quartet on 'Genius'
Jordan Zevon, Ariel Zevon, David Letterman: additional vocals
Producer: Warren Zevon
Recorded at Anatomy of a Heartache Studios, Private Island Studios, Los Angeles; Spike Recording, Pilot Studios, The Ed Sullivan Theatre, New York
Release date: 7 May 2002
Label: Artemis
Chart placings: US:173, UK: 146
Running time: 41:10

Despite its meagre chart positions, *Life'll Kill Ya* put Zevon back in the spotlight, and he was keen to capitalise on this, beginning work on his next album as soon as he returned from his May 2000 European tour. There was only one obstacle: he didn't have any songs.

When it came to writing words and music, he found the words half of the equation torturous, telling Marc Weingarten of the *Los Angeles Times*: 'A lot of the time, it's an awful, unnatural struggle for me to write lyrics. I think of it as a necessary evil'. However, he had a cunning plan to counter this. Over the past few years, he'd made a series of literary connections, whether it was via playing with the Rock Bottom Remainders, striking up a friendship with gonzo journalist and *Fear and Loathing in Las Vegas* writer Hunter Thompson, or through a recent fan letter he received from Irish poet and future Pulitzer Prize-winner Paul Muldoon. Zevon quested about for collaborators and got positive responses from Muldoon, Thompson, previous writing partner Carl Hiaasen, and sportswriter and *Tuesdays with Morrie* author Mitch Alborn.

Thus was born *My Ride's Here*, the second consecutive Zevon album with a title reflecting his preoccupation with mortality. The ride refers to a hearse, and though it's not hugely obvious, that's exactly what Zevon peers out from in the front cover shot. In keeping with the theme, the press release described the album as 'a meditation on death'.

My Ride's Here proves to be an album based more on conceit than concept, and Zevon's great literary experiment rewards him with his patchiest platter since the 1969 debut. There is some strong material – the title track,

'Lord Byron's Luggage', 'Genius' – but the overall disc is scuppered by 'Macgillycuddy's Reeks', 'Hit Somebody! (The Hockey Song)' (surely two of the worst entries in the Zevon catalogue) and the excruciating cover 'I Have To Leave'.

The album divided the critics. *PopMatters* thought it 'an eclectic, catchy opus that equals and occasionally surpasses his last really great release, *Sentimental Hygiene*'. Even Robert Christgau in *Rolling Stone* – no champion of Zevon – gave it three and a half out of five, stating it had 'two crucial improvements on Zevon's honourable 2000 Artemis debut, *Life'll Kill Ya*. First, it rocks harder (and louder); Second, it doesn't dwell much on his love life, which, after decades of dysfunction, we have the right to judge as a not especially interesting permanent disaster area'.

Conversely, veteran reviewer Barney Hoskyns wrote that it lacked 'grit and fire', and even Artemis boss Danny Goldberg was less than impressed, believing 'The album seemed less focused ... than *Life'll Kill Ya*', and that it contained only 'one fully realised song' in 'Genius'.

My Ride's Here reached a healthy 22 in the American Independent Albums chart, but didn't dent any of the majors. Warren had been canned from both Virgin America and Giant after delivering two poor-selling studio albums, and must've been braced for history to repeat itself, but Goldberg still had faith in his artist. That was the good news. The bad news was the inadvertent self-fulfilling prophecy. Zevon had gone to the doctor saying he was feeling kind of rough. The real-life doctor was far less vague than the one in the song. He gave Zevon three months to live.

'Sacrificial Lambs' (Larry Klein, Zevon)

The heavy metal riff that kick-starts 'Sacrificial Lambs' immediately informs the listener that *My Ride's Here* is a different beast from its folk-flecked predecessor. The hard-rocking element is underscored by the presence of 'the Thunder from Down Under', Anton Fig. Although best known as the drummer in David Letterman's house band, the South African first came to attention due to his association with Kiss; he appeared on Ace Frehley's 1978 solo album, subbed uncredited for Peter Criss on all but one track on the Kiss albums *Dynasty* and *Unmasked*, and joined Frehley's post-Kiss combo Frehley's Comet. Fig serves as drummer throughout *My Ride's Here*, and Sheldon Gomberg plays bass.

One might expect an album co-written with several celebrated authors to be a wordy affair, and the six verses of 'Sacrificial Lambs' certainly supports that theory. Zevon's claim that it was 'a spiritual album' also gets early support, with Coptic Monasticism, the Rosicrucian Order, Zoroastrianism, Russian mystic Helena Blavatsky and Indian philosopher Jiddu Krishnamurti all cropping up in quick succession. It's difficult to see the divinity in the penultimate verse, which pairs Iraqi dictator Saddam Hussein and Syrian president Hafez al-Assad with *Smokey and the Bandit* and actor Russell Crowe, respectively, but the narrative gets back on track for the final verse, with science replacing the old religious teachings, and, courtesy of genetic engineering, man replacing God as the maker of men.

Zevon's voice, surprisingly weedy and far removed from the familiar velvet growl, struggles to fit the metal vibe, and the melody is strictly functional, making 'Sacrificial Lambs' the weakest album opener since *Transverse City*'s title track.

'Basket Case' (Carl Hiaasen, Zevon)

The hard-rocking continues with the album's first single, and tied in with Hiaasen's 2002 novel of the same name. The novelist and Zevon had previously collaborated on the *Mutineer* tracks 'Seminole Bingo' and 'Rottweiler Blues'.

> Dracula's daughter, Calamity Jane
> Smoke on the water, water on the brain
> She's pretty as a picture and totally crazed
> My baby is a basket case

These lyrics and the heavy rock approach make it sound like Zevon and Hiaasen are channelling Alice Cooper, and, intentional or not, they succeed. Not only is it easy to imagine the Coop's distinctive rasp delivering these lines, but one also suspects he would do so with greater venom.

The mock baroque chorale halfway through is a surprising enlivener, as is the way the ever-present handclaps suddenly come to the fore after the chorale. Embellishments like these lighten the song up, making it stronger than its predecessor, but it still falls short of being a classic.

'Lord Byron's Luggage' (Zevon)

The mood changes with track three and a return to the folksiness that pervaded *Life'll Kill Ya*. It's the only song credited solely to Zevon on this album, and is one of the highlights.

The title is a literary attention-grabber, but aside from the opening verse, it's less about Byron and more about – surprise! – the nonexistent state of Zevon's love life. Ever the romantic, the singer is 'still looking for love', even though it's like 'Looking for a needle in a haystack', concluding 'Every dog has his day, Jack/I'm still waiting for mine'. So, another from the woe-is-me songbook, but chops must be given to anyone that rhymes 'the Henley Regatta' with *persona non grata*.

Zevon gives this tune an Irish lilt, always a worrying choice when made by a non-Emerald Islander, but he pulls it off pleasingly, concocting a convincing Celtic melody which is further shored up by Katy Salvidge's pennywhistles. The rhythm section is faultless, with Gomberg dropping in an artful bass descend halfway through the chorus, and Fig drumming as if at a military tattoo.

'Macgillycuddy's Reeks' (Paul Muldoon, Zevon)

Zevon remains in Eire for 'Macgillycuddy's Reeks', named for the mountain range in County Kerry. Unfortunately, this sounds *exactly* like a native Angeleno's concept of Irish music, and not even Salvidge's pennywhistles, Fig's bodhran, or the co-authorship of an actual Irishman can redeem this clichéd Celtic cringer.

'You're A Whole Different Person When You're Scared' (Hunter S. Thompson, Zevon)

There's an immediate upswing with this song co-written with gonzo journalist Hunter S. Thompson. Against a backing that is both sinuously cool and borderline sinister, the song dismisses America's long-standing claim to be the Home of the Brave, and rechristens it the Kingdom of Fear. The narrator is so wary of the post-9/11 United States that he leaves his Turkish lover in her native land.

Warren wrote the following in a November 2001 diary entry:

> Hunter came up with a lot of lines for 'You're A Whole Different Person When You're Scared'. 'It's like headline writing!', he exclaimed of the process. Indeed.

This presumably refers to the non-sequitur second verse, which comprises seemingly random phrases such as 'The eagle screams on Friday' and 'The Colts are doomed this year'. Quite how the Indianapolis NFL team's poor 2000/2001 performances contribute to the Kingdom of Fear is never explained.

Kingdom of Fear was also the name given to a collection of Thompson's writings released in book form in 2003.

'Hit Somebody! (The Hockey Song)' (Mitch Alborn, Zevon)

Sportswriter, *Tuesdays with Morrie* author, and Rock Bottom Remainder Mitch Alborn collaborated on the words to the final entry in the informal sports trilogy that began with 'Bill Lee' and continued with 'Boom Boom Mancini'. The backing band on this song is the CBS Orchestra, formerly known as Paul Schaffer & The World's Most Dangerous Band, aka David Letterman's house band for 33 years.

Zevon takes one of his longest songs to tell one of his slightest stories, that of a hockey enforcer, or 'goon', who just wants to score a goal. After 20 years, he succeeds, only to be knocked unconscious by his Finnish counterpart. And that is essentially it. There's a degree of ambiguity in the narrative, courtesy of these lyrics: 'The big man crumbled, but he felt alright/'Cause the last thing he saw was the flashing red light/He saw that heavenly light'. Is the light heavenly because it confirms that the hero Buddy has achieved his career goal? Or is it heavenly because Buddy dies from his injury? Alborn favoured the former, and assumed Buddy would regain consciousness, but Zevon insisted on the bleaker outcome, otherwise the song would've been out of synch with his 'meditation on death'.

'The Hockey Song' is overly long and not terribly interesting, but what brings it truly crashing down is David Letterman's periodic shouts of 'Hit somebody' from the sidelines. Sometimes it's okay to *not* do a famous friend a favour.

'Genius' (Klein, Zevon)

The word genius cropped up every so often in reviews of Zevon's work, but he was too self-deprecating to take such sentiments seriously, even dismissing the notion in the closing lyrics of this song, with the line, 'If I could only get my record clean/I'd be a genius'. In other words, he recognised that he was too flawed, too human, to have that label bandied around about him.

However, with this song, Zevon produced something unique in his catalogue, a pop song where the primary players were a string quartet, and it was his approach to this song that made those who worked on it with him realise that he was something special, something more than the other musicians they'd worked with. *My Ride's Here* producer Noah Scot Snyder:

> He wrote each part by himself and did notation on the computer ... the violins, the viola and the cello. But for Warren to not only know the music, but to be able to write out the parts? It was more than a level of understanding, it was a full level of *knowledge*.

When Katy Salvidge got the call to play on the album, she'd never heard of Warren, telling a friend she was going to work with 'some guy called Lawrence Zevon'. She, too, was quickly impressed with the musician's ability, by the fact he'd written out note-for-note what he wanted her to play on the pennywhistle, by his improvisational ability but mostly by his string arrangement for 'Genius'. As she told Crystal Zevon: 'It was the most unbelievable arrangement I've ever heard. It's probably my favourite string arrangement of all time. It was musically so advanced, and I could tell that he wasn't just a rock and roller'.

The string quartet are wonderful throughout, but especially so when the traditional rock instruments drop off upon Zevon singing the final word, leaving the strings to deliver the coda, gloriously unabetted.

In terms of the words, the familiar lost-love formula is spiced up with added bite. Addressing a former partner who has moved on to someone new, the narrator wonders bitterly if his ex uses the same seduction techniques she did on him – 'Did you light the candles?/Did you put on *Kind of Blue*?/Did you use that Ivy League voodoo on him too?' – before later casting a postdated insult, 'You and the barber make a handsome pair/Guess what?/I never liked the way he cut your hair'.

Interspersed with this is admiration for people the narrator perceives as successful lovers, the song's titular geniuses. First, there's Mata Hari, who had men 'falling for her sight unseen', then Einstein, who was 'making out like Charlie Sheen', and finally, his ex-lover, who 'broke my heart into smithereens', before concluding with the realisation that genius is not a title that applies to him.

The novel musical arrangement and quirky rumination ensures 'Genius' is one of the album's highlights, and should warrant its inclusion in any retrospective of Zevon's work. Indeed, it provided the title for the third and final Zevon retrospective released in his lifetime, the 2002 collection *Genius: The Best of Warren Zevon*.

'Laissez-Moi Tranquille' (Serge Gainsbourg)

'Laissez-Moi Tranquille' – 'Leave Me In Peace' in English – is a relatively obscure Serge Gainsbourg brass-and-percussion-propelled ditty from a 1960 EP. Zevon covers it faithfully, replacing the brass with keyboards. Recruiting daughter Ariel to speak exasperated French over the playout is a nice touch, but Zevon missteps by adding an unnecessary guitar solo and overextending the fade. Perhaps the reason Monsieur Gainsbourg's original clocked out before the two-minute mark was because he understood that *that* was all it required, whereas Monsieur Zevon's forced elongation doesn't do the song, or the listener, any favours.

'I Have To Leave' (Dan McFarland)

McFarland met Zevon in high school in 1962, and they remained friends for the rest of Zevon's life. One can only assume Zevon recorded this song because he genuinely saw merit in it, but compared to Zevon's own impeccable ballads, this is an exercise in banality.

'My Ride's Here' (Muldoon, Zevon)

The title track – Paul Muldoon's second collaboration on the album – leans more towards Zevon's rock and roll roots than Muldoon's Celtic heritage, and in doing so, avoids repeating the cod-Oirish catastrophe of 'Macgillycuddy's Reeks'.

When promoting the album, Zevon was adamant that his literary co-conspirators write the bulk of their songs' lyrics, even telling Muldoon he was 'quite content playing Keith to your Mick'. In a later interview, Zevon said, 'Part of this rather savage criticism I've seen about the album is that people think there is something deeply lazy about collaborating with all these writers, but the simple answer is that I love singing their words'. It can therefore be assumed that the lyrics are primarily Muldoon's. That being the case, he presents us with a dizzying array of biblical, cultural, pop-cultural and western references, though what it all means is frankly anyone's guess. Particularly striking is verse three, which depicts 17th-century poet John Milton warning his 19th-century Romantic descendants Byron, Shelley, and Keats, 'You bravos had better be ready to fight/Or we'll never get out of East Texas tonight'. Ignoring the impossible chronology and the improbable location, it sounds like a Tarantino movie waiting to happen.

Hotels provide a convenient rhyming device and have an inexplicable presence throughout, with the narrator initially 'staying at the Marriott/With Jesus and John Wayne', before ending up at the Westin, where – wouldn't you know it? – 'In walked Charlton Heston'. Milton was staying at the Hilton, of course. Speaking of convenient rhyming devices, the use of 'Jim' in the excerpt 'I believe the seraphim/Will gather up my pinto/And carry us away, Jim/Across the San Jacinto' certainly sounds more like a Zevon line, as 'Jim' had previously popped up in 'Werewolves Of London' and 'Piano Fighter'.

Musically, 'My Ride's Here' aims for the anthemic, the soaring chorus guitar calling to mind the guitar hook from Springsteen's 'Born To Run'. Appropriately, Springsteen opened his first gig after Warren's passing with 'My Ride's Here', though he slowed it down to something more elegiac. That version can be heard on the Zevon tribute album *Enjoy Every Sandwich: The Songs of Warren Zevon*.

The Wind (2003)

Personnel:
Warren Zevon: vocals, piano, keyboard, guitar
Jorge Calderón: bass, guitar, maraca, tres, Spanish vocal on 'El Amor De Mi Vida'
Jim Keltner: drums
Luis Conte: drums, percussion, bongos, congas, maraca
Ry Cooder: guitar on 'Dirty Life And Times'; slide guitar on 'Prison Grove'
Bruce Springsteen: guitar on 'Disorder In The House'
Tommy Shaw: 12-string acoustic guitar on 'Knockin' On Heaven's Door'
Randy Mitchell: slide guitar on 'Knockin' On Heaven's Door'
Brad Davis: electric guitar on 'Knockin' On Heaven's Door'
David Lindley: lap steel on 'Numb As A Statue'; electric saz on 'Prison Grove'
Mike Campbell: guitars on 'The Rest Of The Night'
Reggie Hamilton: upright bass on 'Prison Grove' and 'El Amor De Mi Vida'
Don Henley: drums on 'Dirty Life And Times'
Steve Gorman: drums on 'Knockin' On Heaven's Door'
James Raymond: piano on 'El Amor De Mi Vida'
Gil Bernal: saxophone on 'Please Stay'
Background vocals: Emmylou Harris, Billy Bob Thornton, Dwight Yoakam, Bruce
Springsteen, Tommy Shaw, Randy Mitchell, Brad Davis, Jorge Calderón, John Waite,
Don Henley, Timothy B. Schmidt, David Lindley, Jordan Zevon, Jackson Browne, T
Bone Burnett, Tom Petty, Warren Zevon.
Producers: Jorge Calderón, Noah Scot Snyder, Warren Zevon
Recorded at Cherokee Studios, Anatomy of a Heartache, Sunset Sound, The Cave,
Groovemasters, Henson Studios, Fancyboy, and Masterlink
Release date: 26 August 2003
Label: Artemis
Chart Placings: US:12, UK: 57
Running time: 45:08

It was fate twisting at its most cruelly ironic. Here was a man who, by his own
admission, had 'lived like Jim Morrison a lot longer than he did', and who, as he
told Carl Hiaasen, had in a previous life 'taken so much stuff that could kill you',
that he'd often gone to bed not knowing if he would wake again. Yet he had
survived the dangerous habits and erratic behaviours of his 20s and 30s, had been
sober for sixteen years, hadn't smoked a cigarette in five, went to the gym daily
and worked out for hours, and had now just been handed a death sentence.
   Mesothelioma is a rare form of cancer, usually associated with exposure to
asbestos. Because a single dry fibre of asbestos can enter the system and lead to
mesothelioma years or even decades later, it's speculated that Zevon's cancer
sprang from childhood exposure to the asbestos insulation that lined the attic
of Stumpy Zevon's carpet shop.
   Warren decided to use his remaining time to make an album. In the first
instance, it was what he loved doing, but secondly, it would provide future

financial support for his family. He cannily understood that his illness would make him newsworthy for the first time in decades, so he instructed his manager Brigette Barr to exploit it for all it was worth. Sure enough, all the big guns that had ignored Zevon for years – *Rolling Stone*, *USA Today*, *Billboard*, *The New York Times*, *People* – were suddenly clamouring to interview him. When Danny Goldberg first signed Zevon, he had got in touch with VH1 to see if they'd be interested in devoting an episode of their documentary series *Behind the Music* to his new signing. An executive bluntly told Goldberg, 'Want to know why our viewers won't care? Because I don't'. *Now*, of course, they *did* care, and wanted to document the making of Zevon's as yet untitled final album. Zevon agreed, also green-lighting interviews with the print media named above, and making a final appearance on *The Late Show with David Letterman*. He knew such exposure would help album sales. However, many other media outlets wanted a piece of him, and he knocked them all back. He had a valedictory album to make, and time marched relentlessly on.

'Fame after death is the noblest of goals', says Beowulf in the eponymous Old English poem. Fast-forward a millennium or so, and post-death fame can be measured in sales. A week after David Bowie's 2016 passing, his new album *Blackstar* entered the UK album charts at number 1. This is not surprising, as, by the 21st century, a new Bowie album was rare and, therefore, an event. But what's astonishing is that the same week saw the *Nothing Has Changed* compilation re-enter at 5, *The Best Of 1969/1974* at 11, *Hunky Dory* at 14, *The Rise and Fall of Ziggy Stardust and the Spiders from Mars* at 17, *Best of Bowie* at 18, *Aladdin Sane* at 22, *The Next Day* at 25, and the *Five Years* box set and a staggering ten more albums in the top-100.

Similarly, Freddie Mercury's late-November 1991 death saw 'Bohemian Rhapsody' hit number one again in mid-December, giving rise to the British pub quiz favourite: 'Who are the only band to have a UK number one single with the same song in four different years?'.

Of course, Warren Zevon never compared to these icons in terms of sales or fame, but he was canny enough to recognise the power of impending doom as a marketing tool, and quick enough to come up with quotable copy, such as quipping that he hoped to make it until the next James Bond movie came out, and enquiring whether they still make EPs. *The Wind* was his most successful album since *Excitable Boy*, reaching number 12, sandwiched between 50 Cent and YoungBloodz, and spending 18 weeks in the *Billboard* Top 200. It hit the top spot on the US Independent chart and became his first album to grace the UK Top 100, reaching 57. Meanwhile, 2002's *Genius: The Best of Warren Zevon* made its chart debut the same week *The Wind* peaked, entering at 168, the only week Zevon had two albums in the same chart.

The Wind was nominated for five Grammy awards and won two, Best Rock Vocal Performance (Group or Duo) for 'Disorder In The House', and, bizarrely, Best Contemporary Folk Album, a tag that would've been appropriate for *Life'll Kill Ya,* but ill-fitted *The Wind.* It was a critical success at the time of its release, Sylvie Simmons of *Mojo* being one of many to call it his best, and various magazines and websites such as *Rolling Stone* and *Ultimate Classic Rock* placed it in their year-end lists, with *Uncut* declaring it album of the year.

Would *The Wind* have received all these accolades and attention had its creator not revealed he was terminally ill? In terms of the awards and commercial success, sadly, probably not. But Zevon had always been a critics' darling, so the acclaim would surely have remained. That said, it's a difficult album to review out of context. For example, 'Please Stay' is exquisite, but would its impact have been the same if sung by someone who knew they would make it to Christmas? Is 'The Rest Of The Night' elevated by its irony? Even trying to compare *The Wind* to other Zevon albums can be an exercise in frustration.

It is a strong album, no question, but part of its strength lies in how personal and deeply affecting it is, and as such, it reaches far beyond the autobiography of previous albums. On the one hand, the number of high-quality songs could see it rank alongside *Warren Zevon, Bad Luck Streak in Dancing School, Sentimental Hygiene, Mr. Bad Example* and *Life'll Kill Ya.* On the other, the circumstances of its creation, and the inherent gravitas built into that, means that, to this writer at least, it stands apart. Oddly, it's the poorer tracks, such as 'Numb As A Statue' and 'Rub Me Raw', that make it more a bedmate of the albums listed above, as the one thing Zevon was consistent in was making inconsistent albums.

'Dirty Life And Times' (Zevon)

The budget remained minuscule, but with Zevon and this mortal coil now on nodding terms, music's big guns stepped in to lend a hand. Thus, this song features not only the ever-faithful Jorge Calderón (who will be a huge presence on this album, co-writing seven of the tracks and appearing on all eleven), but also Ry Cooder on guitar, Don Henley on drums, and Dwight Yoakam and Billy Bob Thornton on backing vocals.

Despite this, Zevon's sparkling lyrics ensure he remains front-and-centre, declaring with mordant self-deprecation that he's 'looking for a woman with low self-esteem' to look after him while he's 'winding down my dirty life and times'. Another zinger is 'And if she won't love me, then her sister will/She's from Say-one-thing-and-mean-another's-ville'.

The jocular country tempo, heightened by Yoakam and Thornton's backing vocals and Calderón's fat pumping bass, makes it clear that self-pity is not on the agenda, although the opening line contains a quietly devastating description of terminal illness in 'Some days I feel like my shadow's casting me'. Even more surprising is that it was apparently written pre-diagnosis but ended up fitting the situation perfectly, much as Springsteen's 'My City Of Ruins' became a hymn for 9/11 despite predating that tragedy.

'Disorder In The House' (Jorge Calderón, Zevon)

The fun and feistiness continue with this hard rocker, which presents a searing indictment of the Bush Jr. administration, bizarrely interlaced with descriptions of Zevon's untidy living conditions. It's tempting to think that some of the lines directly reference his mental and physical state, but this was never acknowledged by either of its writers.

The lyric is a true partnership between the friends, with each bouncing ideas off the other like they had when writing 'Mr. Bad Example'. Zevon came up with the title but asked Calderón to start the words. In doing so, Jorge introduced the two themes – 'Plaster's falling down in pieces by the couch of pain' being a nod to the Zevon sitting room, while 'Helicopters hover over rough terrain' presumably references Afghanistan or Iraq. It allows a nice ambiguity to bounce back and forth throughout the song, where the house could at times be the Zevon abode or the White House. There is some wonderful osmosis going on between the two writers in crafting the words, as evidenced by Calderón placing 'reptile' before Zevon's 'wisdom', creating a striking and memorable phrase, or the latter adding 'Even the Lhasa Apso seems to be ashamed' after the former's 'It's a fate worse than fame'.

Calderón loses the gloves when it comes to the overtly political statement, calling the preparations for the 2003 invasion of Iraq 'a flaw in the system' driven by Bush, 'the fly in the ointment (that's) gonna bring the whole thing down'. The later statement that 'The big guns have spoken/And we've fallen for the ruse' surely alludes to the big lie about Saddam Hussein possessing weapons of mass destruction.

Speaking of big guns, this number's guest star is Bruce Springsteen, making a mighty impression with his first appearance on a Zevon record. The Boss lays down some incomparable molten guitar licks while also supplying harmony vocals, and in the case of 'reptile wisdom', counter-harmony. The fun in the studio is evident from the laughter at the end of the track, most especially when Bruce ducks out of singing the 'Lhasa Apso' line, cackling on record, 'I'm gonna let Warren handle that one by himself'.

Springsteen made such an impact on this song that he was rightfully included when it won the Best Rock Vocal Performance (Group or Duo) at the 2004 Grammy Awards.

'Knockin' on Heaven's Door' (Bob Dylan)

When news of Zevon's terminal illness broke, Bob Dylan took to performing 'Accidently Like A Martyr', 'Boom Boom Mancini' and 'Mutineer' on his Never Ending Tour. According to Steve Gorman, who drummed on this Dylan cover, this led to Zevon suggesting he return the favour and that his current circumstances made 'Knockin' On Heaven's Door' an obvious choice. Zevon suggested this at a party at Billy Bob Thornton's house, which had previously been owned by Slash, and still contained the former Guns N' Roses guitarist's Snakepit Studios, now called The Cave. At first, everyone laughed at Zevon's wicked little joke, until they realised he was entirely serious, whereupon they all went to The Cave and got to work. According to Calderón, it was done in one take.

Zevon is backed on this track by an *ad hoc* supergroup consisting of Tommy Shaw of Styx on acoustic guitar, seasoned country musicians and regular Billy Bob Thornton collaborators Randy Mitchell and Brad Davis on slide and electric guitar respectively, Steve Gorman of The Black Crowes on drums, Calderón on bass, and John Waite (The Babys, Bad English), Thornton and everyone else on backing vocals.

Covering the song also allowed Zevon to come full circle; having recorded Dylan's 'If You Gotta Go, Go Now' at the beginning of his career, it seemed fitting he returned to his hero's songbook at the end of it. That said, no one present knew the lyrics for sure, so they transcribed them from a Dylan compilation Calderón had in his car.

On paper, a dying man covering 'Knockin' On Heaven's Door' sounds like a maudlin proposition, but Warren singing from his point of view rather than that of Dylan's fictional narrator transforms the song completely, turning a piece of Western mythologising into a valedictory benediction. Everyone involved performs with a peculiar mix of reverence and aplomb, producing a richly-layered version that's impassioned rather than mawkish. Mitchell and Davis' guitar work is – dare I say it – heavenly, and anyone not moved by Zevon's pleas for that celestial doorway to open up for him has clumsily misplaced their heart.

'Numb As A Statue' (Calderón, Zevon)

The first song recorded for *The Wind* is a perfectly acceptable and pleasant enough tune that restores the upbeat mood the album's two openers established, even as the lyrics find Zevon grappling with his condition. The words place him shortly after his mesothelioma diagnosis, understandably finding the singer overwhelmed, leaving him in the state the title suggests.

The lines, 'I have to beg, borrow or steal some feelings from you/So I can have some feelings too', can, on the one hand, be seen as a typical example of the singer's arch wryness, or as a tacit admission that he'll need the help of others to get through his ordeal. Of course, Zevon being Zevon, he can't resist throwing in a dash of the droll to offset any calamitous sentimentality, telling his emotion donor, 'I don't care if it's superficial/You don't have to dig down deep'.

Though it features some extraordinary lap-steel-playing from David Lindley, 'Numb As A Statue' is strictly in the so-so category compared to the album's stronger tracks, but it did accomplish the all-important task of getting the ball rolling.

'She's Too Good For Me' (Zevon)

This is *The Wind*'s first bittersweet ballad, and portrays that bruised tenderness that Zevon had perfected so well. It represents a complete gear shift for the album in not only being a ballad, but an acoustic number that wouldn't be out of place on *Life'll Kill Ya*. The players number just three, with Zevon on gentle finger-picked acoustic, Calderón on bass, and Luis Conte (Madonna, James Taylor, Jackson Browne, amongst many others) on delicate percussion. Helping to tip the balance on the sweet side are Don Henley and Timothy B. Schmit, who lay down exquisite harmonies.

'She's Too Good For Me' is undeniably lovely, and would stand out on any other Zevon album. But on *The Wind*, it is overshadowed by later ballads that are both lovely and deeply, deeply moving.

'Prison Grove' (Calderón, Zevon)

The acoustic mood remains for this swampy, bluesy dirge in which Zevon indulges in some gallows humour, likening his impending demise to that of a prisoner facing execution. It's the first song on the album where the weakness in Warren's voice first becomes truly apparent, but he is supported by an all-star chain gang comprising Bruce Springsteen, Jackson Browne, Billy Bob Thornton, T Bone Burnett, David Lindley, Jordan Zevon and Jorge Calderón on chanted backing vocals. Ry Cooder adds some slide guitar, simulating the opening line's icy wind, while Jim Keltner adopts an intriguing less-is-more approach, evoking the drudgery of prison life by utilising only the bass drum in the first half of the song, before finally bringing in the full kit on the belated first chorus, but even then playing with funereal restraint.

'El Amor De Mi Vida' (Calderón, Zevon)

'El Amor De Mi Vida' – the love of my life – is the first of the deeply moving ballads referred to earlier. It was begun prior to Zevon's diagnosis and written for and about Annette Aguilar-Ramos, whom Warren had met via Alcoholics Anonymous in the late 1980s. Like many of the album's songs, it took on new meaning in the face of his illness, turning a rumination into a farewell.

The band leader is James Raymond, David Crosby's son, and his sublime piano playing is simultaneously sultry and unbearably sad. He is ably supported by Reggie Hamilton on upright bass, Luis Conte on bongos, and an understated Jim Keltner on drums, who transform the tune into a bossa nova ballad. Calderón contributes Spanish lyrics and vocals, as he did many years earlier on his first Zevon co-write 'Veracruz'. As with the Dylan covers that bookend Zevon's career, there's the sense of a circle being unbroken.

The lyric, started by Zevon but co-crafted with Calderón, is among the singer's most beautiful and, shorn of any autobiographical encryption, it's one of his most direct. Everything is sung from the heart. The opening verse depicts a regretful Zevon haunted by lost love:

I close my eyes, you reappear
I always carry you inside, in here
I fall asleep, you come to me
And once again our love is real

But the second demonstrates acceptance, maturity and selflessness:

I look outside, I know you're there
And you've found a brand new life somewhere
I only wish it had been us
But I'm happy for your happiness

'El Amor De Mi Vida' is utterly heartbreaking and inspiring in equal measure.

'The Rest Of The Night' (Calderón, Zevon)

'Yeah, yeah! Oh yeah! Let's party for the rest of the night!' is a lyric that might be associated more with Kiss than the literate Mr. Zevon, but some fun-filled fluff is precisely what's required to dispel the sombreness of 'El Amor De Mi Vida'.

At face value, this track can be seen as an exercise in bravado, a rock and roll take on not going gently into that good night, even as the lyric knowingly counts down the hours. It could also be viewed as a more-blatant variation on the famous 'Enjoy every sandwich' quote.

Though not in the same class as 'Disorder In The House', this rocker is enlivened by Mike Campbell's surfing guitar bends and backing vocals from chief Heartbreaker Tom Petty.

'Please Stay' (Zevon)

This is not only the saddest song on an album inevitably infused with sadness, but it must be a shoo-in for the saddest song ever written. A weary melancholy pervades every element, be it the sparse arrangement, the rhythm section of Calderón and Conte gently behind Zevon's keyboard, or the words which ache with vulnerability and fear. 'Will you stay with me to the end/When there's nothing left but you and me and the wind' pleads Zevon in a voice wracked with illness, the once-familiar velvet growl present only in an occasional flicker. If Warren's voice is deathly, then Emmylou Harris's backing vocal is positively ghostly, a caressing ethereal presence assuring Zevon he will not be alone. Gil Bernal's emotive sax solo elevates 'Please Stay' to torch song, during which Zevon delivers the album's most poignant moment, a simple 'Oh, sweet darlin'' that is part-sigh, part-prayer.

'Please Stay' is heartbreakingly beautiful, mournful but never maudlin; a devastating masterpiece that is the highlight of *The Wind,* and one of the highlights of Zevon's career.

'Rub Me Raw' (Calderón, Zevon)

If 'Prison Grove' dipped into the blues, then 'Rub Me Raw' jumps in deep, almost to the point of parody with its 'woke up this morning' riff. Despite a fine Zevon vocal and some scorching slide guitar from Joe Walsh, 'Rub Me Raw' is fated to be seen as too bluesy by those that don't like the blues, and too much of a caricature by those that do.

111

'Keep Me In Your Heart' (Calderón, Zevon)
Shadows as harbingers of death bookend *The Wind*. In the opener 'Dirty Life and Times', Zevon felt his shadow was sometimes casting him. Now, ten tracks and months of real-time later, those final 'Shadows are falling and I'm running out of breath'. It's time to say farewell to family and friends, and he does so with this song, a simple heartfelt plea to be remembered fondly, coupled with a resigned acceptance that time will dull that memory.

Death has stalked this album, but never more so than here, in lines such as 'These wheels keep turning, but they're running out of steam', 'If I leave you, it doesn't mean I love you any less' and 'Sometimes when you're doing simple things around the house/Maybe you'll think of me and smile'. Aware that he was indeed running out of steam, Warren had asked Calderón to sing the lead vocal. Calderón was having none of it, recognising that this was Zevon's final artistic statement and that *he* had to be the one to deliver it. To facilitate this, it was recorded at the singer's L.A. apartment, and Zevon managed three vocal takes before being too weak to continue. However, he had done what was required, and *The Wind* was finished. *Media vita in morte sumus* (In the midst of life, we are in death), but the opposite also applies.

Lyrically, 'Keep Me In Your Heart' is faultless. Its purpose is to say goodbye, and it does that with poetical grace. Musically, Calderón's decision to accompany the verses with well-spaced downstrokes on acoustic guitar and Cuban tres lend a droning, dirge-like quality entirely appropriate for a lament, but which is then upstaged by his own richer, livelier arrangement of the middle-eight.

Related songs
'The Christmas Song' (Mel Tormé, Robert Wells)
Incredibly, Zevon was not only able to complete his own album before succumbing to his illness but also contributed to a couple of tracks on *Christmas Moods* (Artemis) by jazz pianist Michael Wolff, who'd previously appeared on Zevon's *Mutineer* and *My Ride's Here* albums.

The first of these is 'The Christmas Song', the yuletide standard first recorded by Nat King Cole in 1946. This is a stripped-back late-night lounge version that's more melancholy than merry. Zevon even came with a backstory to get him in the mood, that of a divorced dad spending Christmas Eve at a bar because he isn't allowed to see his kids. Yuletide cheer it is not.

Accompanied only by Wolff on piano, Warren's vocal weakness is more noticeable, but it arguably makes his delivery more poignant.

'Ave Maria' (Franz Schubert)
'Ave Maria' would prove challenging to most singers at the height of their powers, but here it is painfully apparent that this is far too difficult a piece for a man with besieged lungs. Zevon's voice sounds so much weaker here than at

any point on *The Wind*, making this uneasy listening. One can empathise with Wolff, though; he viewed Warren as one of his dearest friends and probably felt it would be sacrilegious to not use his vocal after the effort the ailing Zevon had put in.

Live, Collected, and Previously Unreleased

Despite his niche status, there's a dizzying array of unofficial live Warren Zevon performances available, mostly on CD, from Amazon and other online retailers. A partial list includes *The Offender Meets the Pretender*, a Dutch radio show from 8 December 1976 starring Zevon and Jackson Browne, featuring a selection of songs from both artists, and a handful of Zevon songs from a concert the following evening; *Nighttime in Chicago* and *Accidentally on Purpose*, both recorded during the 1978 *Excitable Boy* tour; *Headless in Boston*, a 1982 gig that features a cover of Springsteen's 'Cadillac Ranch'; *Things to Do in Cleveland* (1992), which sees Zevon and backing band Odds tackling Van Morrison's 'Into the Mystic', and *The Stone Pony 8/26/94*, a Warren concert from the legendary New Jersey venue. The sound quality of the above ranges from listenable to very good, but ultimately they're all bootlegs. For this reason, this book will look only at Zevon's official live releases, *Stand in the Fire* and *Learning to Flinch*.

Stand in the Fire (Asylum, 1980)

This album was recorded during a five-night residency at The Roxy in L.A. in August 1980, at the culmination of the *Bad Luck Streak in Dancing School* tour. Zevon was joined by guitarist David Landau, who had played on the *Excitable Boy* tour, and a young band named Boulder, whose eponymous 1979 album kicked off with them channelling Graham Bonnet-era Rainbow for a stadium-sized reading of 'Join Me In L.A.'. On *Stand in the Fire*, the Boulder lineup consisted of Zeke Zirngiebel (guitars, vocals), Bob Harris (synthesizer), Roberto Piñón (bass, vocals) and Marty Stinger (drums).

Zevon boldly opened both concert and album with the previously unreleased title song, which is a simple celebration of the joy of performing. Lyrically it's unpretentious to the point of being lowbrow, the subject matter having been tackled more eruditely in songs such as Eric Carmen's 'That's Rock and Roll'. But musically, it's a perfect show-starter, a big slice of melodic 1980s pop that introduces the players and fires up the audience.

The second new Zevon composition is 'The Sin', a stompathon with a strong verse but a woefully ill-defined chorus that sounds several drafts away from completion. The band are terrific, but it is no surprise that 'The Sin' was filed away and quietly forgotten after this tour and album.

The third new track is a medley of two Bo Diddley songs, a strange choice considering they are the self-mythologising 'Bo Diddley' and 'Bo Diddley's a Gunslinger'. The famous Bo Diddley beat is present and correct from the drum intro on, but this is rock and roll from a more primitive time, and sounds it.

Of the more familiar tracks, special mention must go to a rocked-up, full-throated version of 'Werewolves Of London' – during which Warren goes shout-out crazy, name-dropping Brian de Palma, James Taylor and Jackson Browne – and a gloriously passionate 'Mohammed's Radio', replete with then-current references to President Jimmy Carter, the Ayatollah Khomeini, and the ongoing Iran hostage crisis. Hats off to Bob Harris, given the unenviable task of subbing for the studio version's Stevie Nicks, and doing so marvellously. His harmonies a perfect counterweight to Zevon's lead.

Stand in the Fire only received its first CD release in 2007, and it came with four additional tracks, compelling versions of old favourites that make the original platter's inclusion of the leaden Bo Diddley homage even more baffling. 'Johnny Strikes Up The Band', for example, sounds like it really could have them 'rocking in the projects', while 'Frank And Jesse James' is delivered in a voice shot through with Willa Cather weariness.

A double-vinyl 2021 edition added Zevon classic 'Roland The Headless Thompson Gunner', three songs from the under-represented *Bad Luck Streak in Dancing School*, and a superfluous alternative version of 'The Sin'.

Music journalist Paul Nelson – who penned the 1981 *Rolling Stone* cover story detailing Zevon's battle with alcoholism – called it 'The best live rock & roll LP after Neil Young's *Live Rust*', and other reviews were equally favourable, if less hyperbolic. Your current reviewer – no fan of the live document – finds *Stand in the Fire* eminently listenable, particularly the later releases that dilute lesser tracks like the Diddley duo and 'The Sin'. Zevon *is* on fire, and David Landau and the Boulder boys are thrilling throughout. Listening to this, it's difficult to believe that Zevon was already past his commercial peak (*Stand in the Fire* faltered at 80 in *Billboard*, a precipitous drop of sixty places compared to *Bad Luck Streak*'s placing ten months earlier) and that, apart from Bob Harris, who would work with Frank Zappa and Steve Vai, the musicians comprising Boulder would fade into obscurity.

Learning to Flinch (Giant, 1993)

A live greatest hits record released at the height of the MTV Unplugged concert fad might seem like a surefire proposition, but the lack of band, budget and bombast was always going to hobble *Learning to Flinch* as *Stand in the Fire*'s poor cousin. *Learning to Flinch* was stitched together from recordings made during Zevon's solo trek around the globe in 1992 and was less an artistic statement and more a low-cost sales exercise following *Mr. Bad Example*'s poor performance the previous year. The lack of a backing band is the most obvious indicator of the low-to-no budget, and, without the nuances a band can provide, Zevon's rich back catalogue is compressed into two lists, guitar songs and piano songs. An element of sameness inevitably creeps in despite the one-man-band format allowing Zevon to show off his considerable musical dexterity. However, it's the poor production job by Zevon and Duncan Aldrich that is the most devastating flaw, leaving the album sounding like an acceptable bootleg rather than a professional product.

At the time of its release, the album's biggest draws for committed Zevonistas were the three new songs, 'Worrier King', 'Piano Fighter' and 'The Indifference Of Heaven'. Fully rendered versions of the latter two would appear on Zevon's next studio release *Mutineer*, and are reviewed under that album's entry.

'Worrier King' features some excellent bottleneck guitar from Zevon, and the unique arrangement, so swampy you can almost feel the sticky Louisiana humidity, really makes the song stand out. Although a later studio version would've been welcome, 'Worrier King' works well in this format.

There is arguably a fourth new piece, the grandly titled 'Roland Chorale' that introduces 'Roland The Headless Thompson Gunner', but it's just a wash of synthesizer and helicopter sound effects, which, despite the separate track listing, doesn't really qualify it as a new composition. Zevon also inserts an extended musical interlude before the final verse, which, along with the 'Chorale', takes the running time of 'Roland' to just shy of thirteen minutes without ever adding value to the song.

This version of 'Roland' was recorded in Oslo, appropriate for a tune about 'Norway's bravest son', while 'Werewolves Of London' was taken from Zevon's gig at the UK capital's Town and Country venue (now the O2 Forum, Kentish Town). There is none of the name-dropping that populated the *Stand in the Fire* version, though Zevon allows the audience to complete the 'And his hair was ...' line, and their response is 'PERFECT!'.

Elsewhere, there's a slowed-down reading of 'Splendid Isolation' that carelessly misplaces the original's euphoria, a 'Searching For A Heart' stripped of the studio version's lushness, and a reading of 'Jungle Work' that is only one step up the evolutionary ladder from noise. It too comes with the same instrumental padding that plagued 'Roland', but here it fades out before the end, so who knows how much more the poor souls attending the concerts had to sit through. One song that does work well is 'Play It All Night Long', a surprise since it loses both the synthesizer motif and slide guitar that made the original so memorable. To compensate, Zevon provides a piano accompaniment imbued with a traditional 19th-century folk sensibility, and effectively reinterprets the song, rather than just giving it a pared-back acoustic makeover.

Completists will want this album for 'Worrier King', but the casual Warren fan won't find enough here to warrant the investment, and the curious are strongly advised to look elsewhere, as this poorly produced album is an especially poor introduction to one of America's great songwriters. Of all the albums in this book, it is the least essential, though it did return Zevon to the *Billboard* 200 for the first time since 1987's *Sentimental Hygiene*, albeit peaking at a lowly 198.

I'll Sleep When I'm Dead (Rhino, 1996)

This 44-track anthology covers the Asylum, Virgin and Giant years, throws in the hindu love gods' 'Raspberry Beret' for good measure, and remains the most comprehensive Zevon collection to date. Like all good box sets, it includes some previously unreleased tracks to snag the hardcore fan, while providing the impulse buyer with a tempting smorgasbord of prime cuts from all Zevon's releases to date, bar *Wanted Dead or Alive*. One of the unreleased tracks, 'Frozen Notes', later surfaced on the 2007 release of *Excitable Boy*, and is covered under that entry.

'What song provides the unlikely link between Warren Zevon and Abbott and Costello?' is a question unlikely to be asked at any pub quiz anywhere, and the answer is 'You Don't Know What Love Is'. This torch song was written by Gene De Paul and Don Raye for Abbott and Costello's 1941 movie *Keep 'Em Flying*, and was performed by cast member Carol Bruce, but was cut prior to the film's release. Ella Fitzgerald covered it the same year, and Miles Davis, Chet Baker, Billie Holliday, Dinah Washington and Nina Simone are among the many other artists to record it. It's now considered an entry in the Great American Songbook.

Unfortunately, the song's history is far more interesting than Zevon's bloodless interpretation. He sang it at the request of film composer Mark Isham, who used it for the soundtrack of Alan Rudolph's 1990 detective movie *Love at Large*. Isham's own trumpet-playing benefits from the minimalistic arrangement, which simultaneously exposes Zevon's weak vocals. Had Warren deployed his velvet growl, he might've pulled it off, but he attempts some soft-focus singing which leaves him sounding as if he's both lacking in confidence and unfamiliar with the material. That this pallid version made it to the movie's soundtrack is astonishing; that Zevon saw fit to place it on this anthology, doubly so. Happily, the remaining three previously unreleased tracks fare better.

Johnny had a '57 Chevy
With a four-on-the-floor and a 429
We used to take it out onto Wild Horse Pike
Run it out to the end of the line

Anyone with a reasonable working knowledge of American popular music in the last quarter of the 20th century might be forgiven for thinking the above lyrics are lifted from a Bruce Springsteen song. Hats off then to Mr. Zevon, who was asked to come up with a Springsteen-like song for an episode (starring Brad Pitt) of the HBO series *Tales from the Crypt*, and delivered 'Roll With The Punches', every line of which reads like a direct lift from Springsteen's notebook. Musically, it's sturdy stuff that could easily fit with any of the Boss's 1980s mid-tempo rockers, but it *evokes* Bruce's beat sheet rather than mimics it. If the song has a fault, it's the all-too-brief running time.

Speaking of short, the next new song is the wonderfully titled 'If You Won't Leave Me I'll Find Somebody Who Will', taken from the soundtrack of the 1993 television series *Route 66*. A 40-second blast that ends as abruptly as it starts, the ghost of Springsteen lingers in lines like 'I'm a refugee from the mansion on the hill', but this little cracker is recognisably a Zevon original rather than a Bruce pastiche. The only question is whether it should've been developed into a full-length song, or is it perfect the way it is?

The final previously-unreleased song is 'Real Or Not', another soundtrack number, this time from the 1994 series *Tek Wars*. In the liner notes for *I'll Sleep When I'm Dead*, Zevon claims, 'The track reflected my secret fondness for sleazy English techno records', a likely reference to Radiohead, for whom Zevon openly and regularly expressed his admiration. The Oxford band's influence pigments this track, which would not have sounded out of place on *Transverse City*, but is otherwise as far away from Zevon's singular brand of West Coast rock as 'Leave My Monkey Alone' was. As with 'If You Don't Leave Me' Zevon plays all instruments, with Rosemary Butler providing echo-drenched harmony vocals. Like all the incidental television songs, it's both remarkably strong and remarkably brief, clocking in at less than two minutes.

Like any anthology, *I'll Sleep When I'm Dead* will have the listener decrying omissions ('Veracruz', 'Bed of Coals') while bemoaning inclusions ('Poor Poor Pitiful Me', 'Let Nothing Come Between You'). For the uninitiated, however, the collection provides an excellent introduction to Zevon's music, while the presence of 'Frozen Notes', 'Roll With The Punches', 'If You Don't Leave Me' and 'Real Or Not', make it a worthwhile investment for committed Zevon customers.

Preludes: Rare and Unreleased Recordings (New West, 2007)

As the subtitle states, this posthumous release contains a collection of songs receiving their first public airing. There are sixteen songs on the first disc, six of which are brand new to the listener, the other ten being early versions or reworkings of familiar songs, ranging from the lyme and cybelle days to *Excitable Boy*. All sixteen tracks come from reel-to-reel tapes discovered by Jordan Zevon when clearing out his father's belongings and were undated, though it's safe to assume they all predated the 1976 release of *Warren Zevon*. A second disc jumps forward a quarter-century and contains an extended interview conducted when Zevon was promoting *Life'll Kill Ya,* and three songs from that album. It fails to enhance the package one iota and is not required listening.

Disc one's opening track is 'Empty Hearted Town', a previously-unheard piano ballad. What could've been a typical down-on-my-luck story is made atypical by the songwriter's skilful wordsmithery. Zevon was obviously pleased with some of his phraseology here, later recycling 'empty-handed heart' for the song of that name, and 'should'a done, should'a done' for 'Accidentally Like A Martyr'. Musically, 'Empty Hearted Town' is generally representative of the early 1970s SoCal scene, but is not necessarily a song that would've stood out, so perhaps that's why Zevon abandoned it.

'Steady Rain' is more fully realised, being led by an acoustic guitar with support from multitracked keyboards, though the insistent click track running throughout is a clear indicator it is still very much at the demo stage.

'Going All The Way' is a more portentous ballad, one that benefits from an unidentified but very jazzy rhythm section, and could comfortably feature on any of Scott Walker's first four long players.

In the tallest tower of Saint Mary's Basilica in Kraków, Poland, a trumpeter plays a trumpet signal known as the 'Hejnal mariacki', on the hour every hour. It's an unusual piece of music, as it always ends mid-stream, in memory of a 13th-century trumpeter killed by an arrow to the throat while alerting the city to a Mongol attack. I mention this only because I'm reminded of that story every time I play 'Studebaker', the fourth new track on *Preludes*, which ends equally abruptly, mid-word and mid-chord, although, presumably, the reason for this is something more prosaic, like running out of tape. This is a Springsteen car song before Springsteen had car songs, albeit a pessimistic one, for while the Boss's automobiles were born to run and could drive all night and race in the streets, Warren's 'damn Studebaker keeps on breaking down', and the song is a truncated bitchin' session bemoaning this fact. This release was the first opportunity to hear Zevon's original crack at 'Studebaker', but the song itself made its public debut when Jordan Zevon recorded it for the 2004 tribute album *Enjoy Every Sandwich: The Songs of Warren Zevon*.

'Stop Rainin' Lord' is a strum-along folk song, pleasant enough, but the lyrics are slight and the running time short, making it possible Zevon abandoned it before completion. 'The Rosarita Beach Café' is the final 'new' song, a shaggy-dog story in which the protagonist is detained in the titular bar until he pays his tab. The melody has a little touch of Nilsson about it, and if completed, it could have comfortably sat alongside the L.A. stories that populated *Warren Zevon*.

Elsewhere, there are reworkings of earlier tunes ('I Used To Ride So High', 'Tule's Blues'), and early versions and demos of songs from the first two Asylum records. Highlights include: 'Werewolves Of London', which is nicely funked up by an unidentified rhythm section, although the over-the-top grunts and Aargh's that clutter the background rightly sent the song back to the drawing board; a surprisingly up-tempo take on 'Accidentally Like A Martyr' with alternative lyrics; and a more rock and roll delivery of 'Desperados Under the Eaves' that almost equals the finished version.

Preludes is a worthwhile if inessential purchase for the dedicated Zevonista, but the casual fan is instead advised to revisit Zevon's studio releases to plug any gaps in their collection before graduating to this.

Epilogue
Death and Immediate Aftermath

Warren Zevon did get to see the next James Bond film, the couldn't-be-more-appropriately-titled *Die Another Day*. In his excellent Zevon biography, C. M. Kushins relates how Michael G. Wilson and Barbara Broccoli, the producers of the Bond series, upon hearing of Zevon's comment about making it to the next Bond film, arranged for the singer to attend a private screening of the yet-to-be-released movie. This made him only the second person accorded this honour, the first being President John F. Kennedy, who had requested a screening of *From Russia with Love* in the White House shortly after its British release (It wasn't released in the US until May 1964. Incidentally, *From Russia with Love* was only chosen as the follow-up to *Dr. No* because, in a *Life* magazine feature, Kennedy had named the source novel as one of his top ten books).

Zevon did indeed die another day, one that fell long after the three months the doctors had originally given him. He had targets to meet and goals to achieve, and perhaps it was this that gave him the strength to survive for over a year after his initial diagnosis. One of those objectives was to complete *The Wind*, but his daughter Ariel was pregnant with twins, so a more important aim was to be there for her when she welcomed her children into the world. Warren had fallen off the wagon as he wrestled with his illness, but Ariel's pregnancy gave him the necessary impetus to regain his sobriety, and he was there on 11 June 2003 when his grandsons Augustus Warren Zevon-Powell and Maximus Patrick Zevon-Powell were born.

'It's a sin to not want to live', Zevon had said in the VH1 documentary, and he clearly believed that, because still he clung tenaciously to life. As a result, and against all odds, he saw the release of his final work, was read the universally positive reviews, and heard from Danny Goldberg that *The Wind* had shipped gold. One accolade was still not forthcoming, so Warren joked with Crystal that he had better die quickly to secure a Grammy nomination. *The Wind* ultimately received five nominations and won two, but Warren was already gone, having passed away on 7 September 2003, aged 56.

On 8 September, his face stared from the obituary pages of every major British newspaper, an extraordinary circumstance for an artist who had but briefly troubled that country's charts and who'd only toured there twice, most recently to promote *Life'll Kill Ya*, and nearly a quarter of a century earlier supporting Jackson Browne. Sadly, these column inches were less prompted by his art and more to do with his very public approach to bowing out, but the frequency with which the word 'genius' was bandied about in the obituaries and the music press impelled the curious to give Zevon his first and only real British chart success, when *The Wind* reached 57. In the United States, his obituary also appeared in all the majors, but *there* he was a more familiar face thanks to his regular guest status on *The Late Show with David Letterman*, his filling in for Paul Shaffer, his sitcom appearances, his soundtrack work, the time he was part of a celebrity couple with Kim Lankford, that time he spent tearing up the tabloids as the werewolf of Los Angeles, and, yes, even because of his records. Nonetheless, he was undeniably brought back into sharp focus when he announced his illness, and that was always the point.

Because of all or any of these factors, there was the usual knee-jerk buying that inevitably follows a musician's death. But as previously stated, in Zevon's case, this merely meant that *The Wind* cracked the *Billboard* top 20, while the most recent compilation *Genius* flirted briefly with the chart's lower regions. Zevon's postmortem chart success was all too commensurate with his sales while alive.

In the immediate aftermath of his death, Zevon maintained a high profile. The 46th Annual Grammy Awards in February 2004 included a tribute, where Ariel and Jordan Zevon, Jorge Calderón, Jackson Browne, Emmylou Harris, Timothy B. Schmit, Dwight Yoakam and Billy Bob Thornton sang harmony on 'Keep Me In Your Heart', while Warren appeared on big screens singing the lead, in footage from the VH1 documentary. In October that year the all-star tribute album *Enjoy Every Sandwich: The Songs of Warren Zevon* was released, with Springsteen, Dylan, Browne, Don Henley, The Pixies, Steve Earle and others covering Warren's songs. The following year's *Hurry Home Early* featured artists from the more rootsy part of Indietown (Last Train Home, The Matthew Show and others) having a stab at the Zevon catalogue. Meanwhile, Paul Muldoon paid poetic tribute to his friend with 'Sillyhowe Stride': published in his 2006 collection *Horse Latitudes*, and a couple of stanzas Zevon wrote for Ray Manzarek and slide guitarist Roy Rogers before committing to *The Wind* surfaced on their 2011 album *Translucent Blues*, in the song 'River Of Madness'.

There was a flurry of new Zevon product in the years after his death, with the anthologies *Reconsider Me: The Love Songs* (2006) and *Preludes: Rare and Unreleased Recordings* (2007), with 2007 also seeing newly-remastered versions of *Excitable Boy* and *Stand in the Fire*, each complete with a clutch of bonus tracks. The well then appears to have run dry, but the appearance on YouTube of two unreleased songs from the *Sentimental Hygiene* sessions – 'Shadow Of Him' and 'Up On The Cross' – and a much-expanded *Stand in the Fire* for Record Store Day 2021 means that hope springs eternal.

Will The Werewolf Survive?

The song 'Werewolves Of London' will certainly survive. It's securely ensconced in the pop-culture consciousness, a radio favourite at Halloween, and a popular choice for film and television music supervisors. It has appeared in shows as diverse as *House*, *My Name is Earl*, *Community*, *Beavis and Butt-head*, *Glee*, *EastEnders*, *The 100*, *Regular Show*, *Hawaii Five-O*, *Preacher*, *Bless the Harts*, and *Supernatural*, and in the movies *Hoot* (2006) (based on the novel of the same name by Carl Hiaasen), *Grown Ups 2* (2013) and *X-Men: Dark Phoenix* (2019). Other songs have appeared in numerous shows, with *Some Jerk with a Camera*, *Californication* and *True Detective* repeatedly dipping into the Zevon songbook, but 'Werewolves Of London' is the runaway favourite, accounting for approximately 50 per cent of Zevon's soundtrack appearances.

So, the song is secure, but what about the songwriter? On the one hand, there are several artists doing their utmost to ensure that Zevon's music endures, foremost amongst them his most tireless champion Jackson Browne. Browne has included a Warren song in his setlist at most concerts since Zevon's passing, covering not only the material he produced in the Asylum days ('Mohammed's Radio', 'Roland The Headless Thompson Gunner', 'Poor Poor Pitiful Me', 'Carmelita' and 'Lawyers, Guns and Money'), but later songs, including the title tracks of *Mutineer* and *Life'll Kill Ya*. Combine this ongoing tribute with the fact that Browne twice resurrected Zevon's career, then surely one can assume Zevon was speaking in haste when he said David Letterman was the best friend his music had. Browne also appeared as the star guest at Judd Apatow's Warren Zevon tribute nights in 2016 and 2020, along with Dawes frontman Taylor Goldsmith, Jorge Calderón, Jordan Zevon, Jill Sobule, Tim Robbins, Gaby Moreno, Bhi Bhiman and others. (Apatow also curated the 2020 Record Store Day anthology *Warren Zevon's Greatest Hits (According to Judd Apatow)*).

21st-century acts also continue to keep the flame alive, be it Dawes, The War on Drugs, Bhi Bhiman and Madeleine Peyroux, who have all covered Zevon in their setlists; Lucero, who went 'Looking for Warren Zevon's Los Angeles' on their 2015 album *All a Man Should Do*; or The Killers, who have an animated Zevon appear in the video for 'Christmas in L.A.'.

Jackson Browne once told *Rolling Stone*, 'Serious writers, serious lovers of language, will be discovering (Warren's music) for a long time to come', but what if he is wrong? The reality is that Zevon sold only marginally for most of his career, and though he enjoyed a sales spike each time he made a comeback, the numbers soon trailed off again. Age and other distractions will reduce the number of Zevon's loyal customer base further, and despite the efforts of Browne and the artists named above, there's no evidence that this base is being replenished.

There is also Zevon the man to consider. Warren entrusted his biography to his former wife Crystal, and insisted on it being a 'warts and all' portrayal, and she did not flinch. The result, *I'll Sleep When I'm Dead*, depicts Zevon as an abusive and violent drunk, a lifelong and unrepentant philanderer, and a neglectful father (at least when his children *were* children, which is exactly when they needed him most). These behaviours, reiterated in the Kushins biography and in *Always Crashing in the Same Car*, Matthew Specktor's visceral portrait of Los Angeles and some of its former residents, render Zevon a difficult candidate for rehabilitation in the 'Me Too' era.

But this is not to say that Zevon was all villain. Many of those who lived through his 'dirty life and times' (Crystal, Jordan and Ariel Zevon, Jackson Browne, Jorge Calderón) remained loyal and loving to the end, while Zevon, not unaware of his faults, had moments of sweetness and purity. Two examples at the end of his life should suffice. Ryan Raston – who was with him when he died – remembers him calling her in tears, bewildered by his daughter's devotion to him during his illness. 'Why is she here?', he would ask. 'I don't deserve this'. And after meeting his grandsons for the first time, Crystal remembers Zevon tugging her arm: 'I know where the chapel is in this joint. Let's go thank the big guy in the sky'. The chapel door was locked, so they sat on a nearby bench, and Zevon took Crystal's hand. 'This is where we're supposed to be. Don't you see, old girl? We made it. We made it to the front porch'.

Those discovering Zevon for the first time will recognise that though he was a flawed individual, perhaps even deeply so. But if those that knew him could forgave him, then perhaps we that didn't are not best-placed to be so judgemental.

The man is gone, and only his music remains. But with ever less people being exposed to his body of work, time will tell if the lyrics of his last ever song will prove to be prophetic, and we really do only keep him in our hearts for a while.

Bibliography

Avery, K., *Everything is an Afterthought: The Life and Writings of Paul Nelson.* (Seattle Fantagraphics Books, 2011)

Campion, J., (2018). *Accidentally Like A Martyr: The Tortured Art of Warren Zevon* (Milwaukee Backbeat Books 2018)

Charone, B. (1978) 'Warren Zevon: Excitable Boy (Asylum)'. *Sounds.*

Christgau, R. (2002, June 6). 'Warren Zevon: My Ride's Here'. *Rolling Stone* 897.

Cooper, M. (1987) 'Warren Zevon: Rugged Individualism' *Q Magazine*

Ehrlich, D. (1995, May 26). 'Warren Zevon: Mutineer'. *Entertainment Weekly.*

Freeman, H. (2013, August 1). 'Warren Zevon: the man behind the demons'. *The Guardian*

Fricke, D. (2002). 'Warren Zevon and the Art of Dying'. *Rolling Stone.*

Gill, A. (1991) 'REM: The Home Guard'. *Q Magazine*

Gill, A. (1995) 'Warren Zevon's Mutiny'. *Mojo.*

Herzhaft, G. (1992). *Encyclopedia of The Blues.* Fayetteville: University of Arkansas Press.

Hasted, N. (2002) 'Warren Zevon: Life'll Kill Ya'. *Uncut.*

Hasted, N. (2000) 'Warren Zevon: Pictures from Life's Other Side'. *The Independent.*

Himes, G. (1978) 'Warren Zevon: Excitable Boy (Asylum 6E-118)'. *Unicorn Times.*

Joffe, J. (2016). 'How Warren Zevon's Excitable Boy Brings the Horrors of History to Life'. *Observer.*

Kushins, C. M. (2019). *Nothing's Bad Luck: The Lives of Warren Zevon.* New York: Da Capo Press.

Lim, G. (1993) 'Flinching Time: Warren Zevon and the Vast Indifference of Heaven'. *BigO.*

Marsh, D. (1978) 'Warren Zevon on the Loose in Los Angeles'. *Rolling Stone.*

Plasketes, G. (2016). *Warren Zevon: Desperado of Los Angeles.* Lanham: Rowman & Littlefield.

Pouncey, E. (1990). 'Warren Zevon: Transverse City (Virgin America LP/Cassette/ CD)'. *New Musical Express*

Robertson, S. (1982) 'Warren Zevon: The Envoy'. *Sounds.*

Roeser, S. (1995) 'Warren Zevon: Left Jabs and Roundhouse Rights'. *Goldmine.*

Scoppa, B. (1987). 'Warren Zevon: Sentimental Hygiene'. *Creem.*

Simmons, S. (2003) 'Warren Zevon: The Wind'. *MOJO.*

Sullivan, J. (1980) 'Warren Zevon: How L.A.'s 'Excitable Boy' Won the Battle with the Bottle'. *The Boston Globe*

Sullivan, J. (1989). 'Warren Zevon in Hard Times'. *The Boston Globe*.

Wheeler, S. (1990) 'Warren Zevon: Your Guide Through Transverse City'. *Happening*.

Zevon, C. (2007). *I'll Sleep When I'm Dead: The Dirty Life and Times of Warren Zevon*. New York, Ecco / Harper Collins

Zevon, C. (2007). *Living from motel to motel*. Sleeve notes, *Preludes: Rare and Unreleased Recordings*, Los Angeles, New West Records.

Zevon, W. (1996). Sleeve notes, *I'll Sleep When I'm Dead (An Anthology)*, 1996 Elektra Entertainment Group

Websites

Many of the above articles retrieved from www.rocksbackpages.com
www.allmusic.com
www.diaboliquemagazine.com
www.discovermagazine.com
www.debisimons.com
www.insidehook.com
www.loudersound.com
www.musicbox-online.com
www.popmatters.com
www.somethingelsereviews.com
www.theringer.com
www.warrenzevon.com

Also available from Sonicbond

On Track series

Alan Parsons Project – Steve Swift
978-1-78952-154-2
Tori Amos – Lisa Torem 978-1-78952-142-9
Asia – Peter Braidis 978-1-78952-099-6
Badfinger – Robert Day-Webb
978-1-878952-176-4
Barclay James Harvest – Keith and Monica Domone
978-1-78952-067-5
The Beatles – Andrew Wild 978-1-78952-009-5
The Beatles Solo 1969-1980 – Andrew Wild
978-1-78952-030-9
Blue Oyster Cult – Jacob Holm-Lupo
978-1-78952-007-1
Blur – Matt Bishop 978-178952-164-1
Marc Bolan and T.Rex – Peter Gallagher
978-1-78952-124-5
Kate Bush – Bill Thomas 978-1-78952-097-2
Camel – Hamish Kuzminski 978-1-78952-040-8
Caravan – Andy Boot 978-1-78952-127-6
Cardiacs – Eric Benac 978-1-78952-131-3
Eric Clapton Solo – Andrew Wild
978-1-78952-141-2
The Clash – Nick Assirati 978-1-78952-077-4
Crosby, Stills and Nash – Andrew Wild
978-1-78952-039-2
The Damned – Morgan Brown
978-1-78952-136-8
Deep Purple and Rainbow 1968-79 –
Steve Pilkington 978-1-78952-002-6
Dire Straits – Andrew Wild 978-1-78952-044-6
The Doors – Tony Thompson
978-1-78952-137-5
Dream Theater – Jordan Blum
978-1-78952-050-7
Electric Light Orchestra – Barry Delve
978-1-78952-152-8
Elvis Costello and The Attractions –
Georg Purvis 978-1-78952-129-0
Emerson Lake and Palmer – Mike Goode
978-1-78952-000-2
Fairport Convention – Kevan Furbank
978-1-78952-051-4
Peter Gabriel – Graeme Scarfe
978-1-78952-138-2
Genesis – Stuart MacFarlane 978-1-78952-005-7
Gentle Giant – Gary Steel 978-1-78952-058-3
Gong – Kevan Furbank 978-1-78952-082-8
Hall and Oates – Ian Abrahams
978-1-78952-167-2
Hawkwind – Duncan Harris 978-1-78952-052-1
Peter Hammill – Richard Rees Jones
978-1-78952-163-4

Roy Harper – Opher Goodwin
978-1-78952-130-6
Jimi Hendrix – Emma Stott 978-1-78952-175-7
The Hollies – Andrew Darlington
978-1-78952-159-7
Iron Maiden – Steve Pilkington
978-1-78952-061-3
Jefferson Airplane – Richard Butterworth
978-1-78952-143-6
Jethro Tull – Jordan Blum 978-1-78952-016-3
Elton John in the 1970s – Peter Kearns
978-1-78952-034-7
The Incredible String Band – Tim Moon
978-1-78952-107-8
Iron Maiden – Steve Pilkington
978-1-78952-061-3
Judas Priest – John Tucker 978-1-78952-018-7
Kansas – Kevin Cummings 978-1-78952-057-6
The Kinks – Martin Hutchinson
978-1-78952-172-6
Korn – Matt Karpe 978-1-78952-153-5
Led Zeppelin – Steve Pilkington
978-1-78952-151-1
Level 42 – Matt Philips 978-1-78952-102-3
Little Feat – 978-1-78952-168-9
Aimee Mann – Jez Rowden 978-1-78952-036-1
Joni Mitchell – Peter Kearns 978-1-78952-081-1
The Moody Blues – Geoffrey Feakes
978-1-78952-042-2
Motorhead – Duncan Harris 978-1-78952-173-3
Mike Oldfield – Ryan Yard 978-1-78952-060-6
Opeth – Jordan Blum 978-1-78-952-166-5
Tom Petty – Richard James 978-1-78952-128-3
Porcupine Tree – Nick Holmes
978-1-78952-144-3
Queen – Andrew Wild 978-1-78952-003-3
Radiohead – William Allen 978-1-78952-149-8
Renaissance – David Detmer 978-1-78952-062-0
The Rolling Stones 1963-80 – Steve Pilkington 978-
1-78952-017-0
The Smiths and Morrissey –
Tommy Gunnarsson 978-1-78952-140-5
Status Quo the Frantic Four Years –
Richard James 978-1-78952-160-3
Steely Dan – Jez Rowden 978-1-78952-043-9
Steve Hackett – Geoffrey Feakes
978-1-78952-098-9
Thin Lizzy – Graeme Stroud 978-1-78952-064-4
Toto – Jacob Holm-Lupo 978-1-78952-019-4
U2 – Eoghan Lyng 978-1-78952-078-1
UFO – Richard James 978-1-78952-073-6
The Who – Geoffrey Feakes
978-1-78952-076-7

Roy Wood and the Move – James R Turner
978-1-78952-008-8
Van Der Graaf Generator – Dan Coffey
978-1-78952-031-6
Yes – Stephen Lambe 978-1-78952-001-9
Frank Zappa 1966 to 1979 – Eric Benac
978-1-78952-033-0
Warren Zevon – Peter Gallagher
978-1-78952-170-2
10CC – Peter Kearns 978-1-78952-054-5

Decades Series
The Bee Gees in the 1960s –
Andrew Mon Hughes et al 978-1-78952-148-1
The Bee Gees in the 1970s –
Andrew Mon Hughes et al 978-1-78952-179-5
Black Sabbath in the 1970s – Chris Sutton
978-1-78952-171-9
Britpop – Peter Richard Adams and Matt Pooler
978-1-78952-169-6
Alice Cooper in the 1970s – Chris Sutton
978-1-78952-104-7
Curved Air in the 1970s – Laura Shenton
978-1-78952-069-9
Bob Dylan in the 1980s – Don Klees
978-1-78952-157-3
Fleetwood Mac in the 1970s – Andrew Wild
978-1-78952-105-4
Focus in the 1970s – Stephen Lambe
978-1-78952-079-8
Free and Bad Company in the 1970s –
John Van der Kiste 978-1-78952-178-8
Genesis in the 1970s – Bill Thomas
978178952-146-7
George Harrison in the 1970s – Eoghan Lyng
978-1-78952-174-0
Marillion in the 1980s – Nathaniel Webb
978-1-78952-065-1
Mott the Hoople and Ian Hunter in the 1970s –
John Van der Kiste 978-1-78-952-162-7
Pink Floyd In The 1970s – Georg Purvis
978-1-78952-072-9
Tangerine Dream in the 1970s –
Stephen Palmer 978-1-78952-161-0
The Sweet in the 1970s – Darren Johnson
978-1-78952-139-9
Uriah Heep in the 1970s – Steve Pilkington
978-1-78952-103-0
Yes in the 1980s – Stephen Lambe with David
Watkinson 978-1-78952-125-2

On Screen series
Carry On… – Stephen Lambe 978-1-78952-004-0
David Cronenberg – Patrick Chapman
978-1-78952-071-2

Doctor Who: The David Tennant Years –
Jamie Hailstone 978-1-78952-066-8
James Bond – Andrew Wild –
978-1-78952-010-1
Monty Python – Steve Pilkington
978-1-78952-047-7
Seinfeld Seasons 1 to 5 – Stephen Lambe
978-1-78952-012-5

Other Books
1967: A Year In Psychedelic Rock – Kevan Furbank
978-1-78952-155-9
1970: A Year In Rock – John Van der Kiste
978-1-78952-147-4
1973: The Golden Year of Progressive Rock
978-1-78952-165-8
Babysitting A Band On The Rocks –
G.D. Praetorius 978-1-78952-106-1
Eric Clapton Sessions – Andrew Wild
978-1-78952-177-1
Derek Taylor: For Your Radioactive Children –
Andrew Darlington 978-1-78952-038-5
The Golden Road: The Recording History of The
Grateful Dead –
John Kilbride 978-1-78952-156-6
Iggy and The Stooges On Stage 1967-1974 –
Per Nilsen 978-1-78952-101-6
Jon Anderson and the Warriors – the road to Yes –
David Watkinson 978-1-78952-059-0
Nu Metal: A Definitive Guide – Matt Karpe
978-1-78952-063-7
Tommy Bolin: In and Out of Deep Purple –
Laura Shenton 978-1-78952-070-5
Maximum Darkness – Deke Leonard
978-1-78952-048-4
Maybe I Should've Stayed In Bed –
Deke Leonard 978-1-78952-053-8
The Twang Dynasty – Deke Leonard
978-1-78952-049-1

and many more to come!

Would you like to write for Sonicbond Publishing?
We are mainly a music publisher, but we also occasionally publish in other genres including film and television. At Sonicbond Publishing we are always on the look-out for authors, particularly for our two main series, On Track and Decades.

Mixing fact with in depth analysis, the On Track series examines the entire recorded work of a particular musical artist or group. All genres are considered from easy listening and jazz to 60s soul to 90s pop, via rock and metal.

The Decades series singles out a particular decade in an artist or group's history and focuses on that decade in more detail than may be allowed in the On Track series.

While professional writing experience would, of course, be an advantage, the most important qualification is to have real enthusiasm and knowledge of your subject. First-time authors are welcomed, but the ability to write well in English is essential.

Sonicbond Publishing has distribution throughout Europe and North America, and all our books are also published in E-book form. Authors will be paid a royalty based on sales of their book. Further details about our books are available from www.sonicbondpublishing.com. To contact us, complete the contact form there or email info@sonicbondpublishing.co.uk